The OCD Workbook for Food and Eating Fears

Overcome Obsessive Thoughts and Compulsions Using an Integrative CBT and Intuitive Eating Approach

Lissette Cortes, PsyD, CEDS | Katie Jeffrey, RDN

New Harbinger Publications, Inc.

New Harbinger Publications is an employee-owned company.

New Harbinger Publications, Inc.
5720 Shattuck Avenue
Oakland, CA 94609
www.newharbinger.com

Cover design by Amy Shoup

Acquired by Jess O'Brien

Edited by Amber Williams

Library of Congress Cataloging-in-Publication Data on file

FSC
www.fsc.org
MIX
Paper | Supporting responsible forestry
FSC® C008955

Printed in the United States of America

28 27 26

10 9 8 7 6 5 4 3 2 1 First Printing

"Lissette and Katie achieve what may initially seem impossible to readers: they make the journey of healing from obsessive thoughts and compulsions related to eating and food fears feel tangible and achievable. This is the workbook I desperately needed after my diagnosis, when the future felt scary. Readers will gain valuable skills, understanding, and, most importantly, hope that living a full life is possible."

—**Jason Wood**, director of community engagement at the National Association of Anorexia Nervosa and Associated Disorders, and author of *Starving for Survival*

"*The OCD Workbook for Food and Eating Fears* is like an afternoon with your favorite aunt—wise, comforting, nonjudgmental, and filled with practical, kind advice. It doesn't tell you what you should or shouldn't eat, but provides enough direction to help you find the way yourself. The authors have created an indispensable resource for eating disorder professionals, an intelligent guide for individuals investigating their relationship with food, and an essential addition to the field."

—**Jessica Setnick, MS, RD, CEDS-C**, founder of the International Federation of Eating Disorder Dietitians, and author of *The Pocket Guide to Eating Disorders*

"Lissette Cortes and Katie Jeffrey strongly and convincingly advocate for factoring obsessive-compulsive disorder (OCD) knowledge and skills into the recovery plans of the many people suffering from food and eating fears—some openly, others in silence. Anyone wanting their relationship with food and eating to go from war to peace—and to get more out of life—will benefit immensely from engaging with this thoughtful and inspiring workbook."

—**Jonathan Hoffman, PhD, ABPP**, chief clinical officer at the Neurobehavioral Institute, and author of *Stuck*

"This workbook masterfully blends the best of research and humanity. The authors offer evidence-based tools rooted in deep compassion and clinical wisdom, providing readers with a pathway to recovery that feels both effective and profoundly kind. A vital resource for anyone navigating the complex overlap of OCD and eating fears—and for the clinicians who support them."

—**Melanie Smith, PhD, LMHC, CEDS-C**, clinical director of CBT of Central & South Florida, professional development and education chair of the CBT Alliance of Florida, member of the International Association of Eating Disorder Professionals, and coauthor of *The Renfrew Unified Treatment Model for Eating Disorders and Comorbidity*

"This workbook is an exceptional resource for clinicians and clients alike—grounded in evidence-based practices and guided by research informed by leading experts in OCD and nutrition. I especially appreciate how it highlights the power of collaborative care, encouraging each provider to remain within their area of expertise while working in harmony with others. If you have a patient struggling with OCD-related food fears, this is an absolute must-have."

—**Cali Werner, PhD, CMPC,** licensed clinician specializing in OCD, researcher on athlete mental health, and advocate for evidence-based collaborative care

"This workbook offers an engaging blend of education and reflection, guiding readers to build awareness through empowering questions that lift blame and shame. The authors skillfully highlight how diet culture can exacerbate OCD behaviors while providing practical steps to reconnect with values, present-moment thinking, and one's true self. Reading this feels like sitting with a compassionate, skilled therapist and dietitian who helps you build agency over OCD."

—**Shawna Melbourn, RD, CEDS-C, CIEC**, eating disorder specialist, and creator of the course ED for RDs: Eating Disorder Education for Registered Dietitians

"What Lissette Cortes and Katie Jeffrey have achieved with *The OCD Workbook for Food and Eating Fears* is a hard-fought victory for so many individuals who have felt misunderstood for so long. This workbook provides a carefully crafted road map to get you to the core of your food and eating fears while offering evidence-based skills and strategies to help you live a full life. I wholeheartedly recommend it."

—**Michael Sheffield, PsyD**, cofounder of Compassionate Healing Institute, and treasurer of OCD Central and South Florida

"Personally and professionally, I have been waiting years for someone to write this book. This workbook beautifully explores the many creative ways OCD shows up around food and eating, including lesser-known areas like scrupulosity. It explores evidence-based treatments through a practical and deeply compassionate lens, helping readers move toward a life that expands rather than shrinks. Everyone needs this workbook, including clinicians, individuals with OCD, advocates, family members, and beyond. I am so grateful it now exists for our community!"

—**Rev. Katie O'Dunne, DMin,** founder and director of Stick with the Ick, an inclusive community app supporting individuals with OCD, clinicians, and clergy navigating faith and scrupulosity

Contents

Dedication and Acknowledgments

This book goes out to all the courageous individuals who choose to face their fears every day and live a meaningful life on their own terms. Thank you for always being an inspiration and an example that has carried me throughout my own journey. I am grateful for my loved ones who love me for me and encourage me to dream big and take on new challenges. I want to dedicate this book to all the outcasts and misfits who can be themselves and live an unapologetically authentic life.

I am very grateful to the International OCD Foundation (IOCDF) and the National Alliance for Eating Disorders Awareness for creating a space and a welcoming community for clinical training of evidence-based treatments so that folks experiencing OCD and eating disorders can receive effective and compassionate care. I am very grateful for those who continue to make efforts to further our field, sharpen their skills, and research OCD and eating disorders, to better understand and more effectively treat these conditions.

I want to express my heartfelt gratitude for my coauthor, colleague, and friend, Katie Jeffrey. Thank you for your willingness to partake in this project together and put forth your genuine love for and compassion around this work. I truly could not have done this without you, and I know we will continue to do great things together!

—Lissette Cortes PsyD, CEDS

I dedicate this workbook to all those who live with OCD and food and eating fears. I have learned and continue to learn so much from all of you. Your resilience, courage, hope, and strength inspire me. I hope this workbook will provide you with the support and knowledge to cultivate a more peaceful relationship with food, eating, and your body by helping you bring greater awareness, curiosity, and compassion to your food choices, eating behaviors, thoughts, and feelings so you can nourish your body and mind, experience many sparkle moments, and be able to ride the ups and downs of life.

To my colleague and dear friend, Lissette, without whom this workbook would not exist. From whom I have learned and continue to learn from, who challenges me and with whom I am able to be my true self. Your compassion, thoughtfulness, acceptance, and understanding are treasured.

I am deeply grateful to my parents, who have given me unconditional love, support, and compassion throughout my own journey. I am thankful for your unwavering encouragement and understanding.

To my sister, family, and close friends for their support, love, and kindness. I feel seen and heard in your presence. Thank you.

I am also grateful for the IOCDF and ED community as well as OCD and ED clinicians for their passion, advancement of evidence-based knowledge, and for the support they provide to professional colleagues as well as individuals with lived experience and their families.

—Katie Jeffrey, MS, RDN, CSSD, LDN

Foreword

In a world where food is often a source of celebration, connection, and nourishment, it can also become a battleground for those living with obsessive-compulsive disorder (OCD). The unique impact that OCD often has on people's ability to eat without fear has received very little attention—until now. This workbook, *The OCD Workbook for Food and Eating Fears*, is a groundbreaking contribution to the field, one that offers hope, clarity, and healing through integrating a variety of effective therapeutic strategies.

Lissette Cortes and Katie Jeffrey bring together their professional expertise and personal lived experiences to illuminate a path forward for individuals navigating the challenges of OCD and eating-related fears. Their integrative approach—rooted in Cognitive Behavioral Therapy (CBT) and important principles from Exposure and Response Prevention (ERP), Acceptance and Commitment Therapy (ACT), and Intuitive Eating—offers a compassionate and evidence-based framework for recovery.

What sets this workbook apart is its unwavering commitment to honoring the whole person. It does not reduce individuals to diagnoses or symptoms. Instead, it invites readers to explore their values, cultivate self-compassion, and reconnect with their inner wisdom. Through reflective exercises, easy-to-grasp education, and practical tools, readers are empowered to challenge the fears that have kept them stuck and to reclaim a peaceful relationship with food and eating.

This is not just a workbook—it is a companion for the journey. It speaks directly to the courage it takes to face uncertainty, to lean into discomfort, and to choose challenge over avoidance. It validates the pain and complexity of OCD and eating fears while offering a roadmap toward freedom.

Whether you are a clinician, a loved one, or someone personally affected by these struggles, this book will deepen your understanding and expand your capacity for empathy and support. It is a testament to the power of integrative care, the importance of community, and the resilience of the human spirit.

To those holding this book in their hands: You are not alone. Recovery is possible. And this workbook is here to walk beside you and guide you, one brave step at a time.

—Dr. Nicholas Farrell

Courage doesn't always roar. Sometimes courage is the quiet voice at the end of the day saying I'll try again tomorrow.

—Mary Anne Radmacher

Introduction

Facing Food and Eating Fears and Healing Your Relationship with Food

Welcome

Taking the first step to facing your fears and making changes can be challenging. And yet here you are, reading this workbook and completing your first win in your journey. Congrats to you! We are so glad that you are here.

Although not everyone talks about their food and eating fears, this is something a significant amount of the population struggles with. This workbook was written to support individuals just like you who are dealing with these fears. Those who share your struggles often want to make changes to live a full life and they simply do not know where to start.

The focus of this workbook is to provide you with the tools to heal your relationship with food and live a vibrant life. Our goal is to teach you how to face your fears and make more self-supportive choices that align with your values. We want to acknowledge that health looks different for different people, and as you navigate this workbook, we hope that you can discover what health means to you. This workbook will offer you a starting point in how to identify and make the changes you want to see in your life.

Katie's Journey

As a registered dietitian nutritionist, I am passionate about helping and supporting individuals who struggle with both obsessive-compulsive disorder (OCD) and food and eating fears to receive effective and timely treatment. Unfortunately, I lived with OCD symptoms for twenty-eight years before I was properly diagnosed. During the later portion of those undiagnosed years, I now know that I also experienced OCD food and eating fears.

Those years were frustrating and depleting, with many ups and downs. I lived with an almost constant underlying feeling of fear or that something was off, yet I couldn't articulate this unsafe feeling to others. I experienced greater anxiety as well as panic attacks. I sought professional help, but it was ineffective because it did not include exposure and response prevention (ERP) to treat OCD. My life began to grow smaller, and I became more frustrated and disheartened. Why couldn't I get better? Why was I struggling so much?

I finally received the correct diagnosis, which enabled me to seek and obtain effective evidence-based treatment. Through hard work and resilience, my life began to expand. I learned how to better manage OCD symptoms and develop a more peaceful relationship with food. My personal journey planted the seed to help and support others who may have similar challenges. My hope is that individuals who are experiencing both OCD and food and eating fears will receive the proper diagnosis and treatment in a timely manner so that they can fully participate in their lives and thrive.

Lissette's Journey

As a training psychologist, I completed my postdoctoral fellowship at an OCD treatment center. My third training year was a very challenging and stressful time for me. During this year, I developed significant anxiety symptoms coupled with asthma-related challenges. I became highly concerned with my quality of breathing and often checked if I was breathing correctly. I became fixated with how my body was feeling, and later I began to experience panic attacks. My health anxiety began to affect many areas of my life including my eating habits. I was fearful of how certain foods would affect my health and therefore, I became more selective about the types of foods I was eating.

I finally reached out to a therapist who was versed in exposure and response prevention. Through this treatment, I was able to let go of avoidance and checking and become more accepting of my body sensations. This experience opened my mind to how challenging but rewarding it can be to participate in evidence-based treatment. As a clinician with lived experience, I understand that facing your fears is not an easy task. It is a goal of mine to not only provide quality care for my clients, but to allow them the space to become their own experts and best allies.

Our Passion and Mission

Individuals are often placed in either an eating disorder or an OCD diagnostic category without proper assessment of the complexities and the overlap that is present. For instance, many times individuals enter into treatment with concerns about contamination and are diagnosed with OCD without further assessment of their eating patterns. On the flip side, individuals experiencing struggles with their relationship with food and their bodies are diagnosed with an eating disorder without a further and comprehensive assessment of other potential thoughts and behaviors. Both diagnoses are marked by restriction, compulsions, avoidance, checking and safety behaviors, many of which are improperly addressed—the driving force behind your fears is often overlooked.

Throughout this workbook, we provide tools for you to acknowledge and understand what drives your food and eating fears. It is our mission to help you honor your inner wisdom, develop a peaceful relationship with food, feel comfortable in your body, and cultivate a nourishing self-care practice. We believe that staying curious and having compassion for your thoughts, feelings and behaviors are pivotal to cultivating the courage to face your OCD food and eating fears so that you can enjoy ALL food that you love and live a full, vibrant life.

What Are Food and Eating Fears?

Food is an essential component of human existence. From celebrations, holidays and gatherings to daily nourishment and fuel, food is present in many aspects of our lives. Food and eating fears occur when you are feeling anxious, concerned or distressed about experiencing an adverse consequence related to food and/or the experience of eating.

When we struggle in our relationship with food, it can greatly impact our quality of life. It's likely that you are missing out on experiences you want to participate in because of a specific food and eating fear. Maybe you are not meeting friends at a restaurant or going to a friend's house because of this. Perhaps you experience shame or guilt when you throw away food or turn down food someone offered you because it did not feel safe to you. You may also spend a significant amount of time and energy reading labels over and over or spend great amounts of time inspecting your food to ensure that you won't get sick.

You are not alone. We have treated many individuals who experience fears similar to yours. Throughout this workbook, we will share stories of four individuals who have faced their OCD food and eating fears. Our intention in sharing these stories is to offer you examples of what this journey can look like.

Let's take a look at Tasha's story. Tasha experienced contamination fears and the fear of getting sick. When Tasha came to see us, she complained that her world had gotten smaller. She shared how much she missed cooking for and eating with her wife. She also missed eating at her favorite restaurant. Tasha would often engage in self-induced vomiting as an effort to get rid of contamination in her body from the foods she ate. She often felt hungry when she waited for her wife to come home so she could eat and feel safe. Tasha feared that there could be foreign objects in her food or that the food was not handled correctly when prepared and this had been keeping her from living a full life.

Similarly to Tasha, Luke's life had also been limited by food and eating fears. As an aspiring swimmer, Luke was unable to complete practices like he used to because of fatigue, soreness, and cold intolerance. His teammates and coach were also noticing that he was irritable and sad. Luke had become significantly preoccupied with consuming food in "just right" ways. He felt he needed to chew his food a certain number of times before swallowing and have the "right" thought before taking a bite of food. Luke also experienced decision-making difficulties around food choices and needed to be at the "just right" hunger level before he gave himself permission to eat. Luke also experienced additional concerns including a fear of weight gain. As a result of his food fears, Luke's body was not receiving the fuel it needed to perform.

Amber was feeling defeated because she felt her efforts to live a healthy life were no longer working. Amber had attended a school seminar where the presenters spoke about life longevity and nutritional interventions to sustain a "healthier" lifestyle. As a result, Amber started to cut out specific foods, count grams of sodium in her meals, and avoid eating at restaurants and therefore, she only had a few foods she allowed herself to eat. Amber was concerned because high blood pressure ran in her family, and she wanted to prevent this from happening to her. Amber was consumed with distressing thoughts and was afraid of making the "wrong" food choices that could negatively affect her health.

Food fears can also stem from the experience of eating itself. Carlos avoided slimy foods due to his experience of choking on a piece of sushi at age twelve. Carlos was malnourished due to his minimal food intake. He was bothered by textures and smells that resembled sushi or reminded him of his choking experience. Carlos noted that his aversions to certain textures began in his early childhood, making him believe that this would be lifelong, and that he could never get better.

OCD can be very tricky and can affect many different aspects of an individual's life. Typically, the reason it looks different from person to person is because OCD attaches to what each person values the most. From smell and texture aversions to the experience of eating to contamination fears, health concerns, or seeking a "just right" feeling, OCD can manifest as many different types of food and eating fears.

Fears keep you stuck, preventing you from learning and growing. And, if you take fears at face value, you may reinforce them as right and valid. Part of the journey is changing the response you have to your fears, such as embracing uncertainty, leaning into discomfort, and behaving in value-oriented ways. Throughout this workbook, we will dive into how you can change your response to OCD food and eating fears.

Food and eating fears can also be present outside of an OCD diagnosis when the symptoms include fears of weight gain and concerns with changes in body shape and size. Typically, these types of food fears are seen in eating disorder diagnoses. However, these symptoms can also exist in OCD, and there is often significant overlap across diagnoses.

What to Expect: Challenging Food and Eating Fears

When you get stuck in an OCD cycle, you miss out on what you truly value in life. When you do this, it's as if fear is driving your life. In order to get unstuck, it is important to face your fears. This builds your courage. Courage is not the absence of fear but doing something you value in the face of fear. In order for courage to exist, fear must be present.

How do individuals face their fears? In order to answer this question, we have to understand what fuels our fears. In OCD, intolerance for uncertainty is a main contributor to the reinforcement of fears in one's life. Engaging in values-based behaviors despite fear increases your ability to tolerate uncertainty. OCD tends to discourage you from taking action unless you feel 100 percent safe or "just right," which inadvertently reinforces the idea that something is unsafe or dangerous.

In order to challenge a fear, you must accept uncertainty while taking action. Ask yourself: "How do I know it is worth it to accept this uncertainty and take action despite my fear?" How each person answers this might differ. Only you can define this based on your individual values and aspirations. Think about what you hope to gain from doing the work, facing your fears, and improving your relationship with food. You can also consider what led you to pick up this workbook—thinking about your "why" will be an important foundation as you practice these tools.

We believe that a healed relationship with food involves peace, flexibility, imperfection, courage, and self-compassion. Consider what a peaceful relationship with food looks like for you.

Reflection: If you woke up tomorrow and your relationship with food was more peaceful, what would be different? How would you feel? What would you be doing?

____

____

____

____

____

____

The Impacts of Nutrition and Malnourishment on the Brain and Body

Part of our biological make up includes chemicals in our bodies called neurotransmitters that are used by our cells to communicate messages about mood, appetite, and sleep. When we eat, our bodies digest and absorb nutrients such as vitamins, minerals, amino acids, glucose, and fatty acids. These nutrients cross the blood–brain barrier and interact with brain enzymes, which then impact neurotransmitter activity. These nerve chemicals influence brain function, impacting our mental health.

Nutrients impact our bodies and how we function in various ways. For example, and contrary to popular belief, carbohydrates are our friends and not our enemies. They are the preferred energy source for both our brain and muscles. Therefore, carbohydrates are essential for mental and physical energy.

When it comes to protein, this nutrient is in charge of promoting cell and muscle growth and repair, which includes your heart. Amino acids are the building blocks of protein and an essential part of neurotransmitters and hormones. Sufficient carbohydrate consumption is required for your body to be able to use protein to create and repair muscle.

The last macronutrient is dietary fats. Dietary fats are an important energy source and required for maintaining both carbohydrate and protein stores in our bodies. They are carriers of vitamins and are components of hormones. They are excellent sources of the vitamins A, D, E, and K. Additionally, dietary fats help prevent the breakdown of protein for use as a fuel source. Instead, when sufficient dietary fats are consumed, protein can be used to repair and build body tissue. Dietary fats are also valuable because they improve the taste, flavor, texture, and aroma of the foods we eat.

Our body fat serves many purposes including:

- Boosts immunity and reduces inflammation
- Is important for joint, brain, and heart health
- Maintains healthy hair, skin, and nails
- Is required for growth and development
- Regulates temperature and insulates from extremes
- Protects and cushions organs
- Protects, softens, and makes flexible skin
- Regulates hormones
- Facilitates the creation of cholesterol and prostaglandins
- Maintains menstrual cycle and reproductive hormone levels

Below are examples of foods/beverages that are primary sources of each of the above nutrients.

Carbohydrates:

- Grains including rice, bread, pasta, bagels, cereal, oats, and quinoa
- Starchy vegetables such as corn, peas, potatoes, and winter squash
- Fruit and fruit juices
- Legumes (e.g., beans, lentils)
- Milk, yogurt
- Soda and sweetened beverages
- Desserts including candy, cookies, cake, and donuts

Proteins:

- Animal products such as eggs, meat, fish, poultry, lamb, and dairy products.
- Plant-based products, including whole grains, beans, lentils, nuts, and seeds
- Soy foods such as tofu, tempeh, and edamame

Dietary Fats:

- Plant-based foods, including avocado and olives
- Dairy products, such as milk, yogurt, cheese, and butter
- Animal products, including bacon, sausage, and oily fish (like salmon)
- Oils, including olive, peanut, coconut, and canola
- Desserts, including ice cream, cookies, and donuts

You may have noticed that this list is missing certain vegetables such as broccoli, tomatoes, and carrots. This is because they are not a main source of the above macronutrients; however, they are packed with other nutrients including fiber, antioxidants, water, vitamins, and minerals, making them essential to building and increasing your food variety.

One food can often fit into multiple categories; therefore, you may be consuming more nutrients than you think. One of the intentions of making peace with food is to expand your food variety so that you are receiving various nutrients. Feel free to refer back to this list as a reference in helping you increase your food variety as you plan food exposures to challenge your OCD food and eating fears.

All our bodies are different and therefore have varied nutritional needs. If an individual is not meeting their energy needs, every system in the body is affected. The results of under-fueling include:

- Diminished growth and development
- Reduced skeletal muscle function
- Bone health issues
- Hampered gastrointestinal function
- Urinary incontinence
- Reduced neurocognitive function
- Impaired glucose and lipid metabolism

- Decreased energy metabolism/regulation
- Impaired reproductive function
- Reduced immunity

Both under- and overeating can result in poor nutritional status, which can impact appetite, energy levels, sleep, food cravings, mood, and mental health. When your mental health is suffering and you experience anxiety and/or depression, this, in turn, influences your appetite.

Therefore, you can find yourself utilizing food as the only source of meeting emotional needs, resulting in overeating or undereating. You may also find yourself feeling too tired or anxious to plan and prepare meals and snacks, further depleting your energy.

UNDER- & OVEREATING ↔ MENTAL HEALTH ISSUES

Some examples of what you might experience when your nutrition is impacting your behavior and mental well-being may include:

- Poor quality of sleep
- Decreased concentration and focus
- Easily fatigued
- Difficulty engaging in activities for an extended period of time
- Difficulty processing information
- Irritability and impatience

Facing your fears will be harder if your body is malnourished and underfueled. It is not uncommon for individuals to feel frustrated when they find themselves not making the progress they would like in their mental health journey. This is unlikely due to a lack of effort. What you need is to build a foundation by adequately fueling and nourishing your body to give yourself the best chance of improving your mental health.

Here are some signs that could indicate that you are underfueled and/or undernourished when working on exposures and facing your fears:

- Limited cognitive awareness, insight, flexibility, and comprehension
- Forgetfulness
- Poor attention span

- Low motivation or interest
- Difficulty understanding and applying what you learn
- Inability to process anxiety and depression as effectively as when your body is in a well-nourished state.

Reflection: What is an intention you can set to better support your brain and body? Think about food and eating fears you would be willing to face or behaviors you would be willing to change.

____

____

____

____

Working with a Multidisciplinary Treatment Team

When addressing OCD food and eating fears, it is important to consider the whole person, which includes their psychological, nutritional, and medical experiences. OCD food and eating fears can be very complex and therefore, it can be beneficial to have a comprehensive team of clinicians to navigate this journey alongside you.

The Benefits of Working with a Registered Dietitian Nutritionist

It takes time and practice to adequately fuel and nourish your body. Give yourself time. OCD food and eating fears often result in a disconnection from your own hunger and fullness cues, making it extremely difficult to choose food that sufficiently supports and nourishes your body. Nutrition counseling can provide you with support, encouragement, and compassion when facing your OCD food and eating fears.

Below are some examples of how a registered dietitian nutritionist can support you along your journey:

- Cultivate awareness, curiosity, and compassion for yourself, behaviors, patterns, and thoughts regarding food choices and amounts.
- Optimize your energy, mood, and sleep by learning to enjoy all foods that you love without depriving yourself.

- Create a food hierarchy in order to face your feared foods and then devise strategies to begin to face these fears to increase your food variety and enjoyment of eating.
- Develop a personalized and flexible nutrition plan to optimize your overall well-being. This may include hunger and fullness awareness, meal and snack timing and suggestions, how to increase food satisfaction and pleasure as well as nutrition education that can be used as a guideline for making food decisions.
- Work together to help you cultivate a more peaceful relationship with your food and your body.

The Benefits of Working with an Exposure and Response Prevention (ERP) Therapist

When working on OCD food and eating fears, the goal is not just to feel better but to get better at feeling all your emotions and physical sensations. We often experience "negative" or unwanted feelings as something to get rid of. However, the key in OCD treatment is to be willing to participate in otherwise avoided experiences.

The purpose of ERP is to learn new information about your ability to overcome a situation, feeling, or thought you believe could affect you negatively. An ERP therapist can help you identify what you avoid while devising strategies to help you become more confident in facing your fears and therefore enriching your life.

Below are some ways in which working with an ERP therapist can benefit you:

- Help you identify your values and goals
- Offer compassionate care, support, and a nonjudgmental therapeutic space
- Increase your tolerance for anxiety, distress, uncertainty, and/or disgust
- Improve your functioning
- Collaborate with you to face a feared outcome and decrease avoidance
- Explore and challenge the barriers preventing a peaceful relationship with your food and body

The Benefits of Working with a Medical Provider

The consequences of restricting your food intake can significantly affect your body and create a chaotic relationship with food and eating. In the process of reestablishing a peaceful relationship with food, some individuals will greatly benefit from the medical monitoring of a physician. The medical provider can offer valuable information regarding health and overall well-being.

Here are some ways in which your physician can be a strong player on your team:

- Monitor vitals such as blood pressure and heart rate
- Order lab work to check for vitamin or mineral deficiencies
- Assess hormone levels
- Perform different tests to examine organ function
- Track weight range fluctuations, if necessary

Reintroducing nutrients can be a very delicate process that takes time and patience. Individuals who have been malnourished or in a starved state for at least five consecutive days and reestablish adequate food intake too quickly are at risk of experiencing a medical condition referred to as *refeeding syndrome* (Academy of Eating Disorders, n.d., 24). This syndrome occurs when there are dangerously low blood levels of phosphorus and electrolyte imbalances. Refeeding syndrome can affect the neurological, pulmonary, neuromuscular, and hematological functions of the body.

For individuals who might fall into this category, we highly encourage that they speak to a medical provider to assess their possible risk of refeeding syndrome.

The Benefits of Working with an OCD Psychiatrist

Many individuals who have OCD are often faced with anxiety and depression. Anxiety and depression can keep you stuck in an avoidance cycle, making it difficult to overcome your fears or engage in exposure work. Medication can be seen as a "boost" or a way to provide support to your brain and body so that you can be well equipped to engage in your exposures. A skilled OCD psychiatrist can provide you with the best medication to meet your individual needs.

Here are examples of how an OCD psychiatrist can support you:

- Complete an individualized assessment of your mood and levels of anxiety
- Find the correct medication(s) to treat your symptoms (e.g., depression, anxiety, attention deficits)
- Monitor your progress and adjust your medication(s) accordingly
- Help you experience anxiety at more manageable levels

We understand that not everyone may have access to or the means to work with a collaborative team of clinicians. Oftentimes, one clinician versed in these matters can offer substantial support in your treatment. A collaborative clinician might be willing to educate themselves and/or receive supervision from other clinicians outside their specialty or scope of practice to best support you. Your care and support team may involve many different people, from friends to family to clinicians. We encourage you to check out the resources at the end of this workbook to supplement your journey in a way that works best for you.

Potential Members of Your Multidisciplinary Treatment Team

- Psychotherapist, Psychologist, Mental Health Counselor, Social Worker specialized in OCD and/or eating disorders
- Registered and Licensed Dietitian Nutritionist specialized in eating disorders and/or OCD
- Psychiatrist
- Primary Care Provider
- Sports Psychologist or Dietitian
- Athletic Trainer
- Occupational Therapist
- Gastroenterologist
- Endocrinologist
- Occupational Therapist or Feeding and Eating Therapist

Reflection: As you consider your individual needs for your recovery journey, think about who will be part of your care team (e.g., clinician(s), friend(s), family member(s), others). Please list these individuals using the space below.

____

____

____

____

____

Wrapping It Up

Throughout this workbook, you will be provided with strategies and exercises to support you as you face your OCD food and eating fears. You also have access to free tools online at http://www.newharbinger.com/56203. Take this moment to reflect on what you have learned thus far about your relationship with food so you can set intentions for utilizing this workbook.

Reflection: How often will you read this workbook and practice? For instance, will you set aside time daily or weekly? How much time will you devote? What will keep you on track?

____

____

____

Use the chart on the following page to decide what days and times of your week to practice. Remember to exercise compassion and flexibility when you plan out these times. Life happens, and some weeks you might practice more than other weeks. Plan to meet yourself where you are!

Time of Day	Monday	Tuesday	Wednesday	Thursday	Friday	Saturday	Sunday
Morning							
Afternoon							
Evening							

Part 1

Psychoeducation

"I am not fully healed, I am not fully wise, I am on my way. What matters is that I am moving forward."

—Yung Pueblo

Chapter 1

Get to Know Your OCD Food and Eating Fears

It's time to get to know your OCD food and eating fears by taking your first steps toward self-reflection and self-awareness. The goal of this chapter is to help you become your own expert so that you can understand the function or the "why" behind your eating behaviors and food choices. Through self-assessment you will discover the mechanisms of your OCD, including your triggers, obsessions, avoidance strategies, safety behaviors, and other compulsions. Bringing awareness to how your OCD functions will provide opportunities to challenge your OCD and make life changes that are in tune with your values.

What Is Obsessive-Compulsive Disorder?

It is estimated that 1 in 40 adults and 1 in 100 children currently experience *obsessive-compulsive disorder* (OCD) (https://iocdf.org/about-ocd/who-gets-ocd/). According to the *Journal of Obsessive-Compulsive and Related Disorders*, it can take a mean duration of 7.1 years from the onset of symptoms for an individual to receive a proper diagnosis (Hezel et. al., 2022). It is not uncommon that many people first realize they have OCD by learning about it through social media or picking up an OCD book and then tying the information back to their own experiences. This is why self-assessment and self-awareness can be such a powerful first step.

OCD, once known as the *doubting disease*, is a mental health condition that is neurobiologically based and is marked by *obsessions* and *compulsions*. Obsessions are intrusive, unwanted thoughts, images, sensations, urges, memories, ideas, or other experiences that create significant distress, discomfort, anxiety, or disgust. On the flip side, compulsions are behaviors, rituals, or avoidance strategies that people engage in to get rid of, neutralize, undo, or prevent the undesired physiological and emotional experience associated with the obsessions.

Obsessions are intrusive, unwanted thoughts, images, sensations, urges, memories, ideas, or other experiences that create significant distress, discomfort, anxiety, or disgust. Compulsions are behaviors, rituals, or avoidance strategies that people engage in to get rid of, neutralize, undo, or prevent the undesired physiological and emotional experience associated with the obsessions.

Obsessions can stem from different areas of a person's life, including relationships, safety, health, cleanliness, sexual orientation or interests, religion, morality, and somatic experiences. Another way obsessions may present is the concern of reaching a "just right" feeling in order to feel okay. Things may not look, sound, or feel "right" to the individual and therefore, the individual engages in a behavior to attempt to reach a "just right" feeling, perfect feeling, or feeling of completeness. This obsession is centered around relieving discomfort and tension rather than avoiding feared outcomes associated with other OCD themes.

For many, when anxiety, disgust, discomfort, tension, or fear are experienced in one or more areas of their lives (e.g., going through a breakup, coming in contact with germs, finding someone attractive that they feel they shouldn't be attracted to, eating a food that doesn't feel "safe"), a significant urge to fix or mitigate the distress is present. These situations are referred to as *OCD triggers*.

You may be familiar with what these triggers are for you because it is likely that you aim to prevent these situations from occurring or avoid them altogether, seeking relief. These types of behaviors are compulsions. In the long run, avoidance or other compulsions reinforce the meaning, fears, and concerns associated with the obsessions.

There are many themes or symptoms of OCD, and no two individuals experience OCD in the same way. Typically, OCD attaches to or presents in a way that involves what each person significantly cares about in their life. For this reason, as you navigate this chapter, it will be crucial for you to be as honest with yourself as you can. As previously mentioned, the goal is for you to become the expert of your own OCD experience.

OCD Themes and Symptoms that Impact Your Relationship with Food

Let's dive in! You're here because OCD is making your relationship with food challenging. There are many themes or symptoms of OCD, and some of these may apply to you and some may not. The following themes and symptoms typically influence an individual's relationship with their food by affecting their food choices, the way they eat, how much they eat, when they eat, and with whom they eat:

Contamination

- Fear of germs or food spoilage
- Fear of a food causing a feeling of contamination in the body
- Fear of plates/bowls/serving dishes/cookware/utensils not being clean enough
- Concerns with bugs or other organisms being in or on a food/beverage
- Aversion to bodily fluids and/or feces resulting from the digestion of food
- Apprehension around contracting an unwanted trait or personality by consuming a food/beverage (emotional contamination)
- Concerns with the quality of food being consumed (e.g., "pure" or "clean" enough foods, GMO foods, artificial colors or sweeteners, pesticides used when growing the food)

Somatic and Sensorimotor

- Distress associated with how clothes feel on the body
- Hyperfixation on the feeling of swallowing or breathing
- Fear of impaired function or having distressful physical sensations due to experiencing heartburn, stomach cramps, constipation, diarrhea, headache, or becoming bloated
- Preoccupation with energy levels and feeling lethargic

Health

- Concerns with health (e.g., heart function, cholesterol levels, blood pressure and blood sugar), illness, or disease
- Fear of illness or disease indicated by being bloated or having heartburn, stomach cramps, constipation, diarrhea, headache, or migraine
- Fear that consuming a particular food could produce an illness
- Fear of the body changing due to consuming a certain food or amounts of food

"Just Right" Feeling

- Concern of having a "just right" feeling when preparing food—for example, cutting food in a certain way to achieve a feeling of completeness
- Feeling the need to have a "just right" thought before the individual is able to take a bite of food or swallow food
- Avoiding foods that don't meet a certain "just right" feeling because of the texture, taste, smell, appearance, color, brand of the food or how the food was prepared or cooked or by whom
- Feeling the need to eat a "just right" amount of calories, protein, carbohydrates, fats, or micronutrients

Morality/Scrupulosity

- Fear of being a "bad person" if food is not consumed in a specific way
- Concerns of being unethical or inhumane by consuming certain foods
- Fear of offending God if foods are not eaten in certain ways (e.g., outside of typical religious practices)
- Fear of being wasteful by wasting food
- Avoidance of purchasing certain foods due to environmental concerns

Harm

- Fear of choking, an allergy, or other adverse reactions to eating
- Thoughts that harm will come to others or themselves if they eat or do not eat in a specific way
- Fear of harm coming to animals due to particular food choices
- Fear of harming someone by sharing food with or cooking food for them

Disgust

- Aversion to the experience of disgust due to the food's appearance, smell, temperature, flavor, or texture (e.g., when preparing or consuming food)
- Concerns with experiencing disgust when eating in specific settings, with certain individuals or around particular animals or insects
- Fear of disgust when preparing or coming in contact with a particular food

Reflection: The first step in your journey is awareness. Looking over the above lists nonjudgmentally, take a moment to consider which of these experiences resonate with you.

____

____

____

____

____

How Is Your Life Impacted by OCD Food and Eating Fears?

Food and eating fears lie on a spectrum. As you might have noticed above, not every OCD theme applies to you. However, regardless of which theme you might identify with, chances are you are investing a lot of time, energy, and effort to feel safe, just right, or avoid a distressing experience such as disgust. Unfortunately, for most people, this investment of time and energy may never feel like enough.

You know that OCD tends to make your world smaller. This means that the places, people, foods, and experiences you once loved and enjoyed no longer feel safe, decreasing your engagement within these areas of your life. This then leads to an increase in feelings of loneliness, anxiety, depression, frustration, hopelessness, and fear.

Let's take a moment to look at how OCD food and eating fears impact your life. Please take a moment to complete the following questions to gain a better understanding of your thoughts, feelings, and behaviors regarding food choices and eating. As you answer these questions, be gentle with yourself and remember that the intention of this exercise is to increase awareness and gather information.

Purchasing Food: What behaviors do you engage in when purchasing food?

Consider: Do you go to the store or order online? Are there only specific types, brands, colors, textures, amounts, calories, macronutrients, etc. that you feel you "must" purchase or avoid? Do you spend a lot of time inspecting food for insects, bruises, or imperfections? Or do you excessively read food labels or ingredient lists?

____

____

____

____

____

____

Food Preparation: How do you prepare food?

Consider: How do you wash your hands (e.g., length of time, use a particular soap, number of soap pumps)? Are you seeking a feeling of contentment, relief, completeness, or a "just right" feeling when you wash your hands or prepare food? Do you have certain pots, pans, knives, cutting boards, or other cookware that you feel you "have" to use? How do you wash or handle the food you prepare (e.g., gloves, excessive cleaning of food, etc.)? Do you count or measure when preparing or portioning out your food (e.g., certain number of food pieces, calories, macronutrients, grams)?

____

____

____

____

____

____

Type of Food: What do you eat?

Consider: Are there certain foods that you avoid or limit? Are there particular foods that you feel you "should" or "shouldn't" be eating? Do you feel like you need to earn the right to eat your food? Are there foods that feel safer to you (e.g., non GMO, organic, no artificial sweeteners or colors, etc.)? Do you eat packaged or unpackaged food? Can you drink from a bottle you previously opened? Can you only drink from your own reusable water bottle?

Eating Location: Where do you eat?

Consider: Are there particular locations where you feel "safer" than others when eating? Do you avoid certain places, restaurants, friends, or family homes? Do you eat indoors or outdoors? In what room of your home do you eat? Do you feel you have to sit in a particular chair or at a certain table?

Eating Food: How do you eat food?

Consider: Do you prefer using your hands vs. utensils when you eat (e.g., using utensils to eat a slice of pizza, etc.)? Do you use certain types of utensils (e.g., disposable, multiple use, size, style)? Where are you getting them from (e.g., drawer, new package, dishwasher, your own storage area)? Do you eat sitting, standing, or in bed? At what speed do you eat? Do you eat while watching a show or movie, listening to a podcast or music, or while talking on the phone? Do you bring your own food when you eat outside your home?

Eating with others: Who do you eat with?

Consider: Are there people you would rather eat with or who you avoid eating with? Do you prefer to eat alone, in secret, or with others? Are you able to eat foods that other people have prepared, such as family members, friends, or restaurant chefs? Do you have your pet with you when you're eating?

Amounts: How much do you eat?

Consider: Do you reach adequate fullness, or do you tend to stop eating before this point? Do you feel like you need to continue to eat even though you are full? Are you able to step away from food that you didn't eat when you are full? Are there any other rules you follow to determine how much you eat?

Behaviors after eating: What behaviors do you engage in after eating?

Consider: Do you feel the need to move your body or be still after eating? Do you engage in self-induced vomiting after eating? Do you need to eat a certain food, or say a phrase or prayer to "undo" what you ate or prevent a negative outcome from happening? Do you need to distract yourself in some way from the process of digestion? Do you ask others for reassurance regarding what or how much you ate?

Food Inventory Chart

Now that you've learned about how OCD has impacted your food choices and eating behaviors, please take a moment to think about the foods you currently eat, would like to eat, and do not have an interest in eating now or in the future. This will help you have greater awareness of your food variety throughout your recovery journey.

Green: Foods that currently feel "safe" and that you consume on a regular basis	**Yellow:** Foods that you tend to avoid, you have had in the past, and that you might like to have again	**Red:** Foods that you do not eat, have not eaten in the past, or have no desire to ever eat

Exposure and Response Prevention

You have now had an opportunity to reflect on how OCD food and eating fears are impacting your life. Chances are you have noticed that your world has gotten "smaller" because of these behaviors. No one wakes up one day and says, "It would be great to engage in compulsions today!" Yet many feel very compelled to do so. Anxiety, distress, disgust, and discomfort all drive compulsions. As humans, we are wired to avoid pain, and many obsessions can feel very painful or distressing.

Because OCD is neurobiological, obsessions are often felt in the body when distress and anxiety are present. Obsessions can feel very scary, oftentimes experienced as shortness of breath, shakiness, tension, lightheadedness, or other unwanted physical sensations. These sensations are then interpreted in such a way that confirms that there *must* be something negative about a particular thought, image, or sensation, due to the fact that they *feel* so bad or scary.

Let's take a moment to imagine two scenarios. First, imagine you are sitting in your living room at home, reading your favorite OCD workbook, and a lion walks into your living room! Your heart begins to beat faster, you feel your muscles tighten, and you notice your breath quicken. Because of these physical sensations, you interpret this as a dangerous situation and therefore, you respond accordingly by either running away or finding a weapon to protect yourself.

Now, imagine again you are sitting in your living room at home, reading your favorite OCD workbook, and this time a bunny hops through the door. You think to yourself, "How adorable!" You experience a warm feeling in your chest, and you begin to smile. You interpret this situation as nonthreatening and respond accordingly by approaching the bunny and petting it.

In the experience of OCD, there tends to be a faulty alarm system that is present, causing individuals to experience bunnies as if they were lions. Things that typically would be nonthreatening are felt as very alarming, threatening, scary, or disgusting.

When you experience an intrusive thought around a certain situation, idea, or thing and then engage in a compulsion, this reinforces the idea that your experience is as threatening, alarming, scary, or disgusting as it feels or as you experience it in your body. If something isn't threatening, then why would we respond by running?

Throughout your OCD journey, you will learn to make different choices when faced with alarms or experiences that you perceive as dangerous. *Exposure practice* entails facing your thoughts, physical sensations, images, situations, objects, and any other stimuli that provoke anxiety, distress, disgust, or any other adverse experience.

Exposure practice entails facing your thoughts, physical sensations, images, situations, objects, and any other stimuli that provoke anxiety, distress, disgust, or any other adverse experience.

Habituation is the decreased physiological or emotional response that is experienced after a repeated exposure to a particular anxiety-provoking stimulus without engaging in compulsions. The choice to not engage in compulsions is referred to as *response prevention*. After being faced with an anxiety-provoking stimulus many times and not engaging in compulsions (i.e., practicing response prevention), you become more used to the stimulus or trigger and therefore, less afraid of it.

Habituation happens for many individuals, but not all. At times, people continue to experience unwanted emotional and physical responses to the trigger, even though they have faced it many times. If this is your experience, please do not feel discouraged!

Although a bonus in your journey, habituation is not necessarily the goal.

In recent years, the OCD community has recognized the shortcomings of aiming for habituation as the main goal of treatment. It's now known that not everyone habituates and therefore, this can feel discouraging to some. The *inhibitory learning model* of OCD treatment aims to overcome the limitations of the habituation model. The main idea behind inhibitory learning is that two meanings (e.g., a fear-based meaning and a newly formed safety meaning) about a certain stimulus or trigger can coexist. Exposure and response prevention helps create a second, newly learned safety meaning or perception of a stimulus that can result in responding to the stimulus in a more adaptive way.

For example, someone who is afraid of choking may think that sushi is very slimy and could easily get stuck in their throat (fear-based meaning). However, in reality, many people eat sushi every day and the casualties of choking on sushi are minimal. Through ERP, this individual can learn a new safety meaning when they recognize that sushi is relatively safe while simultaneously holding a fear-based meaning of the negative consequences of eating sushi.

This newly learned safety meaning inhibits the fear-based meaning and both exist at the same time. Therefore, we can hold a fear-based meaning and at the same time know that we can eat food that evokes fear because we have learned a new safety meaning about this food through ERP. Consequently, this enables individuals to not miss out on eating their favorite foods even though they might fear doing so. In this case, habituation does not need to happen in order for the person to be able to eat sushi.

Reflection: How do you experience "alarms" that follow intrusive thoughts or obsessions? What physical or emotional experiences are present?

____

____

____

The Role of Compulsions

As previously mentioned, as human beings we are wired to avoid pain. Obsessions and intrusive thoughts often come with a great deal of distress that naturally one would want to avoid, prevent, get rid of, or neutralize. Compulsions are the behaviors that are done for this purpose. Compulsions often provide temporary relief, but in the long run they prolong the distress associated with obsessions. There are many types of compulsions, some more overt and easy to pinpoint, and some more covert and challenging to recognize.

Compulsions often provide temporary relief, but in the long run they prolong the distress associated with obsessions.

Avoidance is a common compulsion for many. Avoidance is a deliberate effort to withdraw or refrain from something undesirable or distressing. Once you start to avoid something, it becomes a snowball effect. In other words, avoidance of a specific situation, experience, or food will eventually include avoidance of many other situations, experiences, or foods, further limiting your food variety and life. Continuous avoidance also increases the emotional and physiological impact that an individual experiences from a trigger or a feared food. Avoidance goes hand in hand with not giving yourself a chance to learn what it would actually be like to experience a particular trigger or food.

Safety behaviors are any behaviors done with the purpose of decreasing distress related to a specific food or eating experience when this situation cannot be avoided. Examples of different safety behaviors around food and eating fears include: carrying a water bottle in case you might choke and need help swallowing, bringing your own food to a friend's house, or bringing antacids due to a fear of experiencing acid reflux at a holiday dinner. These behaviors become like "crutches" that you think you have to depend on in order to get through a distressing situation.

Reassurance seeking is one of the more covert types of compulsions that many people engage in, yet few can identify when it is happening. This may look like asking a friend if the food is spoiled, fattening, "healthy," or otherwise "safe" to eat. In this example, the individual would have difficulty accepting uncertainty around this experience and therefore would seek reassurance in order to consume the food.

Self-reassurance serves a similar purpose. When uncertainty is intolerable and you are seeking certainty, you might tell yourself reassuring statements. Examples of self-reassurance statements performed in efforts to reduce or eliminate uncertainty are: "Even if I eat it, I won't get a stomachache," "I know the food isn't spoiled because my mom ate it," or "It's okay if I eat this only if I go for a run this afternoon." This type of compulsion also gets in the way of building your tolerance for uncertainty. In order to accept uncertainty, the intention is to reduce or eliminate self-reassurance statements.

A final example of compulsions is *checking behaviors* including *mental checking*. There are many different ways to engage in checking behaviors. You may be engaging in checking by inspecting your food for any particles that might indicate contamination before eating it. Checking behaviors may also include examining whether the food package or container has been tampered with or looking at expiration dates over and over again.

Mental checking often involves reviewing situations that were distressing to make sure you were and are still safe. For example, you may mentally check if the lunch you ate was actually free of contamination, if you remembered the expiration date correctly, or whether anyone else at the table ate the same things you did.

It's important to consider that you've done these behaviors as a way of managing distress. These actions provided temporary relief for you in the past, and part of your journey moving forward will include letting go of self-judgment or blame. The important thing is to provide yourself space to do things differently and increase your confidence and ability to tolerate distress. Throughout this workbook, you will learn how to approach these experiences with kindness and compassion.

Reflection: What behaviors do you engage in to decrease or "undo" your anxiety, fear, disgust, or another unwanted physical or emotional experience (e.g., restrict your next meal, exercise more, give yourself reassurance)?

____

____

____

Self-Assessment: Compulsions Inventory

Compulsions actively affect your eating experiences and reinforce the unwanted physical and emotional experiences tied to your obsessions. By becoming more familiar with the types of compulsions you engage in, you can increase your chances of responding to your fears in a different and more adaptive way.

By becoming more familiar with the types of compulsions you engage in, you can increase your chances of responding to your fears in a different and more adaptive way.

For each food and eating fear that you experience, use the chart below to list different compulsions that you engage in when faced with this fear. If you're unsure where a particular compulsion goes, not to worry, simply place it where you feel it fits best. The main point is that you take this change to become aware of all of the behaviors that you are engaging in that prevent you from eating the foods you love. As you complete this chart, notice what shows up for you. If recalling certain experiences leads to distress, it is important to note that awareness is a powerful step to facing your fears. By completing this exercise, you're building courage.

Food Fears	Why is this distressing?	Avoidance	Safety Behaviors	Reassurance (From others or self)	Checking
Ex: Eating Sushi	Ex: Food is slimy and I could choke	Ex: Not eating foods that feel "unsafe"	Ex: Carrying a water bottle	Ex: Asking a friend if the food is safe to eat	Ex: Inspecting the food to make sure it's "safe"

Creating Space Between OCD and Your True Self

It's not uncommon for individuals to confuse or intertwine OCD with their *sense of self.* This can make it difficult to differentiate between their own thoughts, values and goals and OCD's goals. OCD tends to be *ego-dystonic* (i.e., not aligning with your sense of self) while your own thoughts, values and goals tend to be *ego-syntonic* (i.e., in sync with your sense of self). At times, it can help to look at OCD as something separate from your sense of self. This allows you to defuse your sense of self from OCD, thereby increasing your ability to challenge and create a more peaceful relationship with OCD.

The following activity will help you begin to see OCD as separate from your sense of self.

Activity: Imagine that OCD is standing in front of you—what does it look like? What shape, color, and form does it have? Is it a human form, an imaginary character, or a creature or an abstract shape? How does OCD talk to you? What type of voice does it have? Is it loud, soft, irritating, or angry? What might you call your OCD? Some individuals give it a human name, others make up a name, and still others simply call it OCD. What best resonates with you?

____

____

____

____

____

____

Finding Your Core Fears

Determining your *core fears* is pivotal to your exposure practice because it will enable you to understand why you engage in compulsions. A core fear is the most underlying fear that is at the root of your distress, anxiety and/or disgust, which drives your OCD thoughts and behaviors. Finding your core fears is powerful because it can help make sense of thoughts, emotions, and behaviors that otherwise seem very random or nonsensical. This will provide the information required to create exposures that will truly be effective in helping you expand your food variety, increase your enjoyment in eating, and live a more fulfilling life.

A core fear is the most underlying fear that is at the root of your distress, anxiety and/or disgust, which drives your OCD thoughts and behaviors.

Here are examples of common core fears in OCD that drive compulsions:

- Death and dying (oneself or others)
- Not trusting the self
- Contracting an illness, cancer, etc.
- Not tolerating one's size/accepting one's body
- Feeling vulnerable
- Feeling distress that will persist forever
- Offending God
- Acting on unwanted sexual impulses
- Being responsible for harm to others
- Being a "bad person"
- A loved one or others contracting an illness, cancer, etc.
- Judgment
- Loss of control
- Rejection by others
- Judgment by others or not fitting in
- Unworthiness or "not enough" thoughts
- Being alone

Discovering Your Core Fear Activity

To help you uncover your core fears, please take a moment to complete the following activity.

Here is an example using Amber's story from the introduction to walk you through this exercise. Amber was limiting foods she felt would increase her blood pressure and was also afraid of making food choices that would contribute to this health outcome.

- What is a fear that is affecting your food choices or amounts and eating behaviors?

  Amber: I am afraid of consuming too much sodium.

- What behaviors do you engage in that you feel would prevent this fear from happening?

  Amber: I choose foods that have no to minimal amounts of sodium. I always check labels and my food app for sodium contents at the beginning of every meal. I don't eat food over a certain amount of sodium that would feel unsafe.

- If you didn't engage in these behaviors, what do you think would happen?

  Amber: My blood pressure would be out of control.

- If this was true, then what would this mean?

  Amber: I would feel scared that I was harming my body.

- If this was true, then what would this mean?

  Amber: It would mean that I am not taking good care of myself or my health.

- If this was true, then what would this mean?

  Amber: I would not live a high-quality life, and it would be my fault.

- If this was true, then what would this mean?

  Amber: I am a careless person and can't trust myself.

- Based on what you considered through this exercise, what do you notice is the core fear at the root of your anxiety and distress that drives your OCD thoughts, emotions, and behaviors?

  Amber's core fear: Fear of not making the right choice for myself and my health.

Now, it's your turn. Please take a few minutes to answer the questions below to explore and discover your core fear. Feel free to repeat this exercise using different compulsions to see if you may have one or more core fears. Some individuals find that their OCD food fears stem from a single core fear, while others recognize that their OCD food fears are driven by multiple core fears.

- What is a fear that is affecting your food choices or amounts and eating behaviors?

___

___

___

- What behaviors do you engage in that you feel would prevent this fear from happening?

___

___

___

- If you didn't engage in these behaviors, what do you think would happen?

___

___

___

- If this was true, then what would this mean?

___

___

___

- If this was true, then what would this mean?

___

___

___

- If this was true, then what would this mean?

____

____

____

- If this was true, then what would this mean?

____

____

____

- Based on what you considered through this exercise, what do you notice is the core fear at the root of your anxiety or distress that drives your OCD thoughts, emotions, and behaviors?

____

____

____

Life Pie Activity

To wrap up this chapter, please reflect on the different areas of your life that you tend to dedicate time, energy, and emotion to. Remember that when OCD gets in the way of living the life that you want, this means that the amount of time, energy, and emotion that you want to devote to certain areas of your life often shrinks. For example, when eating at restaurants is scary to you, you're less likely to go out to eat. Therefore, the time you spend with friends decreases since you don't join them when they go to restaurants.

Visualize the amount of time, energy, and emotion you are devoting to various areas of your life. These areas might include social time, exercise, studying, working, sleeping, or hobbies. Utilizing the first circle below, create a pie chart to represent each of these areas. Each area will be a "pie slice" within the circle. The areas to which you devote more time and energy will have a bigger "slice" of the pie than others. Allow yourself to have fun with this activity! Perhaps choose different colors or patterns for each pie section.

On this second pie chart, take a moment to reflect on how you would ideally distribute your time, energy, and emotion in the areas of your life from the above exercise. Points to consider: Would you need to make some slices smaller to allow other slices to be bigger? Would you want to include a new slice of something else in your life?

Reflection: Now that you have had a chance to reflect on how you show up in your life, you may have a greater understanding of how you want to proceed with your recovery journey. If you could wave a magic wand and wake up tomorrow with the ability to manage and challenge your OCD food and eating fears, what would be different? What would you be doing? How would you be feeling?

Reflection: What might be getting in the way of making these changes happen? How has self-criticism and judgment made this more difficult for you? Be kind to yourself as a dear friend would as you complete this reflection, recognizing that you are worthy of love and kindness.

"The reality of where you are, is always more important than the ideal of where you imagine you should be."

—Jeff Warren

Chapter 2

Your Relationship with Food

Chapter 1 explored how thoughts, behaviors, and emotions tied to OCD impact your food choices and relationship with food. However, there are many more factors that can influence and affect the way you eat and the food choices that you make. This chapter will explore how your environment, culture, nutrition information and knowledge, internal body experiences, and body image can also impact your relationship with food.

Diet Culture

You have probably heard the term *diet culture,* but what does this really mean? Across the globe, the act of dieting tends to be a significant experience for many. The word diet can have different meanings from culture to culture. The definition of diet simply refers to the foods and drinks that someone regularly consumes. In essence, it is a neutral term that our culture has associated with weight loss and restriction of certain foods. You have probably heard someone say, "I am going on a diet," when they refer to cutting down or cutting out specific foods.

Diet culture stems from a set of cultural beliefs and myths that equates health with thinness and criticizes certain foods and eating behaviors. Diet culture also glorifies restrictive eating patterns, fad diets, the idea of "self-control," and "perfect" eating standards. Diet culture ignores our genetic blueprint and uniqueness while emphasizing leaner, more muscular bodies and thinness. In actuality, bodies come in all shapes and sizes and genetics plays an important role in how we look. There is no one "right" or "perfect" way to fuel and nourish our bodies because we are all unique and each of us has different needs.

Diet culture stems from a set of cultural beliefs and myths that equates health with thinness and criticizes certain foods and eating behaviors. There is no one "right" or "perfect" way to fuel and nourish our bodies because we are all unique and each of us has different needs.

Diet culture has a black-and-white perspective. It states that if you follow these strict sets of rules, beliefs, and practices around eating, you are doing it "right" and are "successful" and "good." On the other hand, when you don't adhere to them, it's assumed that you have "failed" or are "bad." These specific sets of rules are created with the idea that the goal is to change your body and be thin.

Those who adhere to a diet culture perspective assume that following these rules correlates with hard work, dedication, discipline, and self-control. This is seen as an achievement or standard of superiority. Diet culture then attaches a sense of worthiness to thinness. For this reason, many experience guilt and shame regarding what, when, how, and how much they eat when it does not follow diet culture's rules.

Reflection: How has diet culture influenced your relationship with food?

____

____

____

____

Good and Bad Foods

As human beings, many of us strive to do the "right" thing most of the time. Diet culture has taken this human aspiration and turned it into a strict rule that designates that there is a right and wrong way to eat. This greatly aligns with the way OCD impacts the way we eat because OCD also creates a black-and-white way of looking at things. In other words, both OCD and diet culture only allow for two polarized perspectives. At times, in efforts to fuel and nourish ourselves adequately, we label foods as "good" or "bad" in order to identify the "right" choice and be successful. This is an example of black-and-white thinking that can also look like, *Did I succeed or fail?* or *Did I do it "right" or "wrong?"*

The OCD themes and symptoms you experience, covered in chapter 1, impact how OCD attaches to how you label foods. For instance, if you experience contamination OCD, "good" foods might be those that are washed or packaged and feel clean or safe while "bad" foods are those that might have bugs in them or be expired. If you experience harm OCD, you might label "bad" foods as those that could bring a negative consequence to yourself or a loved one. Another reason you may label foods as "good" or "bad" could stem from a fear of your body changing. It is essential to be aware that although this fear might exist outside of OCD fears or doubts, it is just as important to address.

Individuals often give into the compulsion of labeling foods as "good" or "bad" because they are seeking certainty, safety, superiority, or morality when they eat the "correct" foods. As previously mentioned, giving into OCD compulsions fuels your OCD food fears similarly to when you follow diet culture's rules. It is unhelpful to label foods as "good" or "bad" because this is often a compulsion which only increases the food fears you experience.

This compulsion is also unhelpful because in the long run, these messages become more meaningful and are internalized. Consequently, we feel that we are "good" or "bad" based upon what, when, how, and how much we eat. Diet culture teaches us that there is only one right way to fuel and nourish our bodies, and this is often reinforced by OCD compulsions. Following strict rules eventually teaches your brain and body that you can no longer trust yourself.

Activity: In the following chart, write down the foods that you may label as "good" or "bad."

"Good" Foods/Beverages	"Bad" Foods/Beverages

Inner and Outer Wisdom

One of the main goals of this workbook is to help you foster a more peaceful relationship with food and your body. Following diet rules leads to mistrusting yourself and creating chaos around your food choices and eating behaviors. Regaining the trust you may have lost is possible by reconnecting and listening to your individual needs. This can be achieved by dropping the black-and-white thinking regarding what, when, how, and how much you're "supposed" to eat. Listening to your *inner and outer wisdom* enables you to drop the black-and-white perspective because wisdom is your own personal experience combined with your knowledge.

Listening to your *inner and outer wisdom* enables you to drop the black-and-white perspective because wisdom is your own personal experience combined with your knowledge.

We have found that most individuals have knowledge regarding nutrition; however, due to diet culture, they have lost their ability to recognize what we refer to as *inner wisdom*. Inner wisdom is having the awareness of how certain foods, amounts of foods, and the timing of meals and snacks affect how you feel emotionally and physically. When you first begin to challenge diet culture, it is difficult to recognize and be aware of your body's signals regarding your needs.

For instance, it can be challenging, at first, to tap into your hunger and fullness cues, thirst sensations, energy levels, and the types or amounts of foods that would be best for you. Yet with practice, your ability to listen to and honor your inner wisdom becomes louder and louder and eventually almost second nature. By learning to see foods as fuel, nourishment, and enjoyment, you can listen to your inner and outer wisdom and view foods in a neutral way.

It's also important to understand and learn how best to listen to and honor your outer wisdom. Outer wisdom is the knowledge of accurate nutrition information as opposed to diet culture's beliefs and myths. Outer wisdom also includes information you learned from your past personal experiences regarding how your body has previously responded to what, when, how, and how much you have eaten. Similar to your inner wisdom, your outer wisdom is unique to you and your experiences.

In the beginning, it can be very challenging to discern or tease apart what is inaccurate or diet culture-influenced nutrition knowledge and what is evidence-based nutrition knowledge. Balancing outer and inner wisdom is pivotal to cultivating a peaceful relationship with food and your body. This increases your ability to identify choices around food and eating that work for you based on your inner and outer wisdom.

To help you begin to understand and recognize inner and outer wisdom, let's use Luke's example from the Introduction. Luke, a swimmer, has been limiting his food intake due to OCD food fears and a fear of weight gain. After completing a hard two-hour practice during which he didn't eat or drink anything, he decided not to go to lunch with his teammates because he wasn't feeling hungry. An hour later Luke began to recognize that he was feeling extremely tired and was having difficulty concentrating on his schoolwork. He noted that he was not experiencing physical stomach sensations of hunger, but he recognized that his low energy and inability to focus were likely due to not eating since breakfast.

Due to this recognition, Luke decided to listen to his inner wisdom (i.e., lack of energy and concentration) and his outer wisdom (i.e., the awareness that he hadn't eaten since breakfast). Even though he wasn't experiencing stomach hunger, Luke chose to fuel and nourish his body. He used his sports nutrition knowledge to build a meal that was both satisfying and adequately refueled and rehydrated his body.

After eating, Luke noticed that he felt more energetic and was more productive when finishing his schoolwork. Reflecting on this experience, Luke realized that he would like to begin experimenting with fueling and nourishing his body soon after practice versus waiting an hour. Luke noted this would better align with his inner and outer wisdom.

Reflection: Think of a recent experience you had with eating. How might you have used your inner and outer wisdom to make choices regarding your food and eating?

____

____

____

____

____

____

Dismantling Diet Culture

Understanding your inner and outer wisdom is a foundation for cultivating an *intuitive eating* practice. The term *intuitive eating* was created by registered dietitians, Evelyn Tribole, MS, RDN, and Elyse Resch, MS, RDN, in their 1995 *Intuitive Eating* book. Intuitive eating uses an inner and outer wisdom approach that challenges the diet culture idea that there is only one right way to eat.

Intuitive eating focuses on meeting your physical and emotional needs by eating in response to hunger, fullness, pleasure, overall satisfaction, and cravings instead of calories or rules. When you practice intuitive eating, you pay attention to your physical and emotional needs and stay curious about why, when, what, how, and how much you eat.

This approach involves taking the focus off of the scale and achieving thinness. Instead, it places the attention on how your body feels when eating certain foods, hunger and fullness levels, the timing of meals and snacks, the taste of food as well as the enjoyment of food and the overall eating experience. Intuitive eating encourages you to listen to and honor your inner and outer wisdom rather than rules, diet culture's myths or OCD food and eating fears.

This practice also emphasizes finding enjoyable ways to move your body and how these activities make you feel both physically and emotionally. By shifting the focus away from variations in your weight and achieving a certain body shape and size, you can more easily tune into your body's wants and needs. Intuitive eating offers you a more compassionate stance when you're building a peaceful relationship with food and your body rather than listening to the chaos that OCD creates.

Intuitive Eating Self-Assessment

These ten principles are the foundations of an intuitive eating practice (Tribole and Resch 2017). Intuitive eating is a practice that you return to repeatedly. It is not about perfection or reaching a finish line. The intention of this workbook is to provide you the opportunity to align your eating behaviors and food choices with the principles of intuitive eating as best as possible.

Take a moment to think about your current experiences of eating. Consider how well you listen to your inner and outer wisdom and how diet culture may influence your eating behaviors and food choices. How much do you agree with the following statements? Please check in with yourself as you answer these statements and offer yourself compassion as you complete this assessment. Take this as an opportunity to gather information and learn the areas that you may want to make changes in.

Statements	Strongly agree	Agree	Neutral	Disagree	Strongly Disagree
I do not follow diet culture's rules.					
I notice when I am hungry and eat at this time.					
I have a peaceful relationship with food.					
I reject rules regarding what, when, how and how much to eat and choose what works best for me.					
I honor my fullness level and reach a level that works for me.					
I choose foods that I love to eat and are satisfying.					
I have different ways to cope with feelings and do not just rely on food.					
I provide my body with what it needs by treating it with respect and kindness.					
I engage in enjoyable movement.					
I rely on accurate and evidence-based nutrition knowledge to make food choices as needed.					

Reflection: Now that you've completed this assessment, take a few moments to reflect on what you noticed as you were completing it. Were you surprised by any of your responses? Was it difficult to assess any of these behaviors? Please be gentle with yourself as you complete this reflection. You are gathering information to learn more about yourself so you can decide how you may want to change your current behaviors moving forward. There is no perfect way to eat intuitively.

____

____

____

____

Utilizing Intuitive Eating to Challenge OCD

In order to build a peaceful relationship with food, it's important to use your inner and outer wisdom and engage in an intuitive eating practice rather than be guided by OCD food and eating fears. When you are practicing intuitive eating, you are aligning with your own individual expertise rather than listening to OCD.

OCD can create a chaotic relationship with food and go against intuitive eating. You are very likely to overlook your body's needs when you focus on relieving anxiety, distress, fear, disgust, or another unwanted experience that stems from OCD. Through an intuitive eating practice, you can challenge OCD by connecting and listening to your inner and outer wisdom despite experiencing unwanted thoughts or physical sensations.

Let's revisit your intuitive eating self-assessment and consider how an intuitive eating practice can help you face your OCD food and eating fears. Please take a moment to complete the following exercise. At this time, you may not have examples for all of these scenarios. If you don't, please name an intention you may want to set for yourself in these areas.

1. Reject the diet mentality: When were you able to challenge your OCD by making food choices that were not based on diet rules, counting amounts, limiting your food intake, or wanting to lose weight?

   ____

   ____

   ____

2. Honor your hunger: When have you allowed yourself to eat when you were hungry even though you were experiencing OCD food and eating fears?

____

____

____

3. Make peace with food: When did you give yourself unconditional permission to eat foods that OCD said were "bad" in some way or not "clean" enough?

____

____

____

4. Challenge the food police: When did you challenge OCD food rules or opinions that stated that you did something "bad" because you ate a certain food or that you're "good" for choosing a certain food?

____

____

____

5. Discover the satisfaction factor: When was the last time you allowed yourself to eat a food that you enjoy very much but otherwise would have avoided because OCD said it was not "safe" in some way?

____

____

____

6. Feel your fullness: Think of a time when you were able to identify that you were comfortably full and made a choice to stop eating despite not achieving a "just right" feeling, not completing a "certain number" of bites, or needing to complete "the right amount of macros." On the other hand, when have you given yourself permission to continue to eat in order to reach

comfortable fullness despite OCD food and eating fears that typically prevent you from reaching this fullness level?

7. Cope with your emotions with kindness: When was a time that you allowed yourself to feel anxiety, distress, disgust, or another unwanted experience and still chose to nourish and fuel your body?

8. Respect your body: Can you think of a time that you respected, felt gratitude toward, or didn't criticize your body? Describe when you were able to make choices that aligned with your body's needs despite fears that your body may change or be negatively affected according to OCD fears.

9. Movement—feel the difference: When was a time you listened to your body and chose movement that you truly enjoyed despite OCD rules around what you were "supposed" to do, what was the "right" activity to engage in, how much was the "right" amount of movement, or the "correct" intensity level?

10. Honor your health—gentle nutrition: Describe a time when you honored accurate nutrition knowledge and your own experiences and decided to fuel and nourish your body accordingly despite what OCD food and eating fears were telling you to do?

Hunger and Fullness Assessment Scale

The hunger and fullness assessment scale is a tool to help you stay curious and become aware of your intentions and choices regarding eating behaviors, foods, and beverages. This scale represents the range of hunger to fullness that you experience. This rating system is purely subjective and very personal. It can help you to get in touch with your body's internal signals which, at times, you may overlook because of OCD.

This is an opportunity to practice exploring how you experience different levels of hunger and fullness. To help you pause and gather information, it will be valuable to tap into your inner and outer wisdom. Let's start by examining your inner wisdom as it relates to your hunger and fullness cues. Ask yourself the following questions and jot down some ideas.

What is my body telling me at this moment? Am I physically hungry (i.e., empty stomach, irritable, difficulty concentrating or low energy due to needing to fuel and nourish my body), or am I hungry for another reason (i.e., wanting to eat because I am feeling a certain way)? Am I feeling tired, stressed, restless, bored, happy, content, grateful, or something else?

Now, let's examine your outer wisdom as it relates to your hunger and fullness cues. Ask yourself the following questions and make some notes.

What and how much have I had to eat and drink today? How did I feel after eating these foods and amounts of foods? When did I eat today and how did this influence my hunger and/or fullness levels?

Using the hunger and fullness assessment scale below, take a moment to practice identifying where you are on this scale (Tribole and Resch 2017). This is an opportunity to identify what you are feeling and get in touch with your body's internal signals. There are no right or wrong answers. This is a tool to learn more about how you experience different levels of hunger and fullness.

Painfully Hungry	Ravenous	Very Hungry	Hungry	Slightly Hungry	Neutral	Slight Fullness	Comfortable Fullness	Slightly Past Comfortable Fullness	Very Full	Painfully Full
0	1	2	3	4	5	6	7	8	9	10

Below are descriptions to help you understand what the numbers mean:

0. **Painfully Hungry:** Primal hunger which feels very intense and urgent.
1. **Ravenous:** Extremely hungry, experiencing irritability and feeling like you can't wait to eat. You don't care what you eat, you just need food.
2. **Very Hungry:** You want to eat immediately and are very eager to do so.
3. **Hungry:** A gentle and polite hunger. You would like to eat, and you could also wait longer.
4. **Slightly Hungry:** You notice your first desire for food and your stomach is moderately empty.
5. **Neutral:** You're not hungry or full.
6. **Slight Fullness:** You feel the food in your stomach without feeling comfortable fullness.
7. **Comfortable Fullness:** You feel satisfied, noting your body has received what it needed.
8. **Slightly Past Comfortable Fullness:** You feel slight discomfort, but it hasn't progressed to an unpleasant experience.
9. **Very Full and Uncomfortable:** Your clothes feel tight, and you feel uncomfortable. You may feel sleepy and sluggish.
10. **Painfully Full, or Stuffed:** You experience pain and perhaps nausea due to experiencing significant fullness.

The point of this scale is to gather information and stay curious so that you can learn your own personal way of how to best fuel and nourish your body. It can be beneficial to check in at different times of the day to identify your needs based on your inner and outer wisdom. The intention of an intuitive eating practice is to increase your overall awareness regarding your hunger and fullness levels, body's needs, thoughts, physical sensations, and emotions. This will allow you to make choices based on your own needs and intentions versus choices based on what OCD requests of you.

Reflection exercises: Challenge yourself to let go of OCD's rules regarding food and eating. What food and eating choices can you begin to experiment with that align with an intuitive eating practice? How can you take the first step with kindness and compassion? Being kind and compassionate to yourself means letting go of self-criticism, perfectionism, and rigidity.

Being your own expert in challenging your OCD food and eating fears means that you understand what works best for you despite OCD. This chapter reviewed how environment, culture, nutrition information and knowledge, internal body experiences, and body image play a role in your relationship with food. Because we each have different needs, there is no right way to eat. By learning about your inner and outer wisdom, checking in with your hunger and fullness cues, and being mindful and intuitive about your eating behavior, you are reshaping the way you make food choices outside of OCD and diet culture. You get to define your own relationship with food, and it doesn't need to look like anyone else's.

Who you are, what your values are, what you stand for, they are your anchor, your north star. You won't find them in a book. You'll find them in your soul.

—Anne M. Mulcahy

Chapter 3

Values-Driven Behaviors

As you navigate your OCD journey and gear up to face your food and eating fears, you are probably thinking about the goals you would like to achieve. This chapter will help you define what is important to you so you're able to identify the reasons for choosing your goals, which will be the guiding force in your journey. This journey is about learning how to live a values-driven life and not about reaching a finish line.

There's a pivotal difference between *goals* and *values*. Goals are concrete and succinct. They focus on the outcome and are often defined by achievement or failure. You either complete or conquer a goal or you don't, which is a black-and-white and rigid way of thinking. On the other hand, exploring the role of values in your OCD food and eating fears journey will allow you to have a more flexible, personal, and compassionate way to tune into your progress.

Values will be your guiding force in this journey. They are like your northern star or compass for how you want to live your life. They are unique to you and what you desire. Values are *ego-syntonic* because they align with your sense of self (i.e., inner and outer wisdom). They are how you want to behave as a human being and define how you want to act on a continuous basis. Therefore, making choices that are values-driven is a practice that you return to again and again.

Goals are concrete and succinct. They focus on the outcome and are often defined by achievement or failure. **Values** are how you want to behave as a human being and define how you want to act on a continuous basis.

Values are different from goals in that they are not finite. When you engage in values-driven behaviors, you let go of the idea that there is a finish line to cross or an endpoint to reach. Instead, you navigate life in a more fulfilling and flexible way.

Below is a list of the most common values. All of them may not resonate with you. There is no such thing as a right or wrong value; it's about finding the ones that are unique to you. Remember, each of us has different values. Read through the list below and put a check mark on the category next to each value (e.g., very important, important, not important). Many individuals find it helpful to choose three to ten values that most resonate with them.

Value	Very Important	Important	Not Important
Acceptance: to view things as they are without trying to change them and apply this openness to myself, others, life, etc.			
Adventure: to actively seek, create, or explore new, stimulating, exciting, and/or thrilling experiences			
Assertiveness: being honest and direct when standing up for my rights and requesting what I want			
Authenticity: to be genuine and true to myself			
Caring: sharing or showing kindness and concern toward myself, others, the environment, etc.			
Compassion: to offer kindness to myself or others in the face of suffering			
Connection: to cultivate closeness; to resonate and engage fully with others			
Contribution: to help, assist, produce, or make a positive difference together with other people			
Cooperation: to collaborate, assist, and work with others			
Courage: to show up or persist in the face of fear, threat, or difficulty			
Creativity: to be innovative; to create novel ideas or think about tasks or projects in a new way			
Curiosity: to be open-minded and interested and take a nonjudgmental perspective; to explore and discover			
Equality: to treat others as equal to myself, and to view myself as equal to others			

Value	Very Important	Important	Not Important
Expressiveness: to share my thoughts and feelings through my actions and words			
Flexibility: to go with the flow and adjust to changing circumstances			
Freedom: to feel unrestrained from the burdens of expectations and rules			
Friendliness: to be inviting and warm toward others			
Forgiveness: to pardon or make a decision to accept another individual's or my own wrongdoing, mistake, or error			
Fun or Playfulness: to seek, create, and engage in pleasurable, enjoyable, or entertaining activities			
Generosity: the spirit and action of freely and frequently giving to myself or others			
Gratitude: to be deeply appreciative of our experiences and the individuals in our lives as well as what means the most to us			
Growth: to advance or improve in knowledge, skills, personal development, or life experience			
Helpfulness: to be ready and willing to assist others			
Honesty: to be truthful and sincere with myself and others			
Humor: to see and appreciate the amusing aspects of life			
Humility: to be modest; freedom from pride or arrogance			
Independence: to be self-supportive; to decide to do things on my own terms			
Intimacy: to experience closeness, understanding and safety in my personal relationships			

Value	Very Important	Important	Not Important
Justice: to uphold fairness and equality			
Kindness: to be considerate or nurturing toward myself or others			
Love: to act affectionately toward myself or others			
Mindfulness: to be aware of, nonjudgmental of, and curious about my present experience			
Open-mindedness: to see things from different perspectives; to stay curious and be willing to consider ideas and opinions that are different from my own			
Patience: to wait calmly for what I want; to continue to do something despite difficulties			
Persistence: to persevere despite problems or difficulties			
Pleasure: to create and give joy to myself or others			
Respect: to be polite, considerate toward myself or others; to avoid interfering with or intruding upon others			
Responsible: to be trustworthy, reliable, and accountable for my actions			
Romance: to show and express love or strong affection			
Self-awareness: to be cognizant of my own thoughts, feelings, and actions			
Self-care: to be aware of and look after my well-being in order to get my needs met			
Spirituality: to recognize the feeling, sense, or belief that there is something greater than myself			
Supportiveness: to be encouraging and available to myself or others			

Value	Very Important	Important	Not Important
Trust: to be loyal, faithful, sincere, and reliable to myself or others			
Vulnerable: to be open and emotionally exposed during times of uncertainty and risk-taking			
Insert your own unlisted value here:			
Insert your own unlisted value here:			

Now that you have identified your top values, please take a moment to list them here:

____

____

____

____

____

Mapping Out Your Path and Direction

The following reflection questions are examples of intentions discussed in this workbook. Let's see how Tasha answered this reflection question based upon her values of connection, adventure, self-care, and acceptance. Tasha experiences fears and concerns around contamination and the possibility of getting sick.

Example **Reflection:** How are one or more of my values a guiding force to face my OCD food and eating fears?

Value: Connection—Being able to eat holiday meals with my family despite the type of food served and eating at restaurants with my friends.

Value: Adventure—Trying out a new restaurant and new foods with my friends. Eating foods that I once loved but am now afraid to eat due to OCD food fears.

Value: Self-care—Being able to resist the urge to make myself throw up even after I think that the food I ate was contaminated in some way. Eating and drinking consistently throughout the day despite OCD food fears.

Value: Acceptance—Accepting not being certain if the food is expired/spoiled and eating it anyway.

Now, take a moment to reflect on your values from the previous activity and think about how one or more of your values are a guiding force to challenging your OCD food and eating fears. In the last reflection of this activity, please fill in the blank with an intention that is personal to you.

Reflection: How are one or more of my values a guiding force to face my OCD food and eating fears?

Value: ______________________________

Value: ______________________________

Value: ______________________________

Value: ______________________________

Reflection: How are one or more of my values a guiding force to have a more peaceful relationship with food?

Value: ______________________________

Value: ______________________________

Value: ______________________________

Value: ______________________________

Reflection: How are one or more of my values a guiding force to respect my body, engage in self-care behaviors, and honor my needs?

Value: ______________________________

Value: ______________________________

Value: ______________________________

Value: ______________________________

Reflection: How are one or more of my values a guiding force to fuel and nourish my body adequately and consistently?

Value: ______________________________

Value: ______________________________

Value: ______________________________

Value: ______________________________

Reflection: How are one or more of my values a guiding force to ______________________?

Value: ______________________________

Value: ______________________________

Value: ______________________________

Value: ______________________________

Cultivating Courage by Behaving in Values-Driven Ways

As discussed in the Introduction, courage is not the absence of fear, but doing something in the face of fear. In order for courage to exist, fear must be present. You are making a courageous choice when you engage in a values-driven behavior vs. engaging in a compulsion or safety behavior driven by fear. Knowing what your values are will help you challenge your OCD food fears.

When you are choosing values-driven behaviors, you are not allowing fear to dictate what you can or can't do. Instead, your actions are guided by your values and inner and outer wisdom. Choosing behaviors that are values-driven entails prioritizing what matters to you, following through with a commitment, exercising integrity, or practicing consistency. Engaging in these types of behaviors cultivates courage, enabling you to face your OCD food and eating fears. Therefore, when you make values-based choices to face your fears, you gain self-confidence in your ability to act despite fear.

Motivation vs. Willingness

Motivation is feeling enthusiastic, ready, or wanting to do something. On the other hand, *willingness* is choosing to do something despite how you feel. Therefore, motivation is based on how you feel about something, whereas willingness is about taking committed action.

Motivation is feeling enthusiastic, ready, or wanting to do something. Willingness is choosing to do something despite how you feel.

Motivation is often thought to be an important factor in determining what you are able to do or not do. Even though motivation can be valuable, it is not the most necessary or useful factor in determining your actions. Just like your emotions, motivation fluctuates from time to time, day-to-day, even hour-to-hour. For instance, let's say you cook a meal for yourself and feel motivated to face a feared food, but then you experience anxiety and poof your motivation is gone. Due to a change in your motivation, you decide to no longer eat the feared food.

Willingness, on the other hand, is steadier than motivation. Willingness goes hand in hand with your values, and values do not typically change rapidly. For example, if you value connection and have plans to eat out with your friends, it is unlikely that your value of connection would all of a sudden not be important to you.

Because you value connection, this will drive your willingness to see your friends even though you are feeling anxious and nervous about eating at a restaurant due to your food fears. Therefore, you check in with your values and decide not to cancel plans despite your anxiety and low motivation. Being willing means that you behave in values-driven ways despite how you feel.

Being able to complete a presentation for a class while experiencing distress and anxiety is one example of how someone might exercise willingness. Even though the student feels nervous to give her presentation, she is willing to do so because she values learning and personal growth. The student is willing to experience distress and anxiety in order to complete something that matters to her.

When you tap into willingness, you allow yourself to feel distressing physical sensations and emotions so that you can do something that matters to you. This also increases your confidence and ability to tolerate distress. Overtime, motivation, emotions, and physical sensations lose their significance in how you determine what you choose to do or not do.

Being willing means that you behave in values-driven ways despite how you feel. Overtime, motivation, emotions, and physical sensations lose their significance in how you determine what you choose to do or not do.

Reflection: What is something you have not wanted to do or have not felt motivated to do and you did it anyway?

Reflection: How might you tap into your willingness to face a food and eating fear this week?

Next Steps

Now that you've had a chance to identify the values that are unique to your experiences, you can choose to act in values-driven ways. Although motivation will change from moment to moment and day to day, your values are more consistent. It is unlikely that they will change as rapidly as the feeling of motivation. Utilizing your values and leaning into your willingness will allow you to better challenge your OCD food and eating fears and move forward in your journey.

Life isn't about waiting for the storm to pass. It's about learning how to dance in the rain.

—Vivian Greene

Chapter 4

Mastering How You Think, Feel, and Behave

Let's take a moment to recap what you have learned so far. You gained knowledge about the importance and benefits of letting go of OCD rules regarding food and eating. You have learned how to make choices that align with your values instead of listening to OCD. You have practiced how to make choices based on your needs and not on society's or OCD's perspectives. You now have a better understanding of how engaging in an intuitive eating practice fosters greater awareness regarding your body's signals. As a result, attending to your values and listening to your hunger and fullness cues and inner and outer wisdom allow you to make choices that align with your needs.

But what if you feel you made a mistake in this process? A big takeaway from this workbook is that there is no perfect way to navigate your healing journey. Every experience is a learning experience; there is no right or wrong way to do it. You are simply gathering information and learning more about yourself and how best to meet your needs. Making "mistakes" is part of the process and not the exception.

Making Room for Perceived Mistakes

Through an OCD lens, life is black and white. In this way of thinking, actions, decisions, thoughts, and choices are perceived in binary ways—as either right or wrong. Oftentimes, because something feels off, wrong or unsafe, we perceive it as a mistake. But in reality, life is full of gray areas, and choices do not need to be so dichotomous.

When it comes to challenging OCD and healing your relationship with food, there are many gray areas that are part of the healing and learning process. In order to move through this process, it is essential to make room for experimenting, flexibility, and making mistakes.

Activity: Think of your favorite color and then think of a friend whose favorite color is different from yours. Who chose the right color? Which color is the best? You did not make yourself like this particular color, but it just happens to be your favorite. Similarly, this is probably how your friend feels about their favorite color. There might be more than one "right" color, even though both colors feel different for each person. When you pick a certain color, it's only right or wrong based upon your perception. It can only be perceived as a mistake when there is a rule that only one color is worthy of a favorite status.

In this example, you are choosing a certain color to be the right one based on how it feels. If you begin to doubt how you feel, then you might question if it was the right choice. As you learned in chapter 1, OCD's rules are feeling based (e.g., fear, anxiety, disgust, discomfort, distress). OCD has you draw conclusions and make choices based on how things feel rather than how they actually are. When you interpret a physical feeling as catastrophic or scary, you feel you have made the wrong choice.

When you experience uncertainty coupled with distress, it can feel as if you have made a mistake. Being uncertain about the color you chose can feel as if you picked the wrong color. Uncertainty feels intolerable, and you feel as though you have to fix your perceived mistake or do something perfectly in order to fix this feeling and get it "right." Being better able to tolerate this feeling helps you make values-driven choices when faced with these false alarms or experiences that you perceive as dangerous, unsafe, or wrong.

Thinking Errors in OCD

The way we think influences how we feel, and the way we feel influences how we think. The following are patterns of thinking that impact how we perceive and interpret physical sensations and feelings. These patterns are based on the faulty alarm systems that are experienced due to OCD. The following is a list of the most common faulty ways of thinking or *thinking errors* in OCD:

1. **Intolerance of Uncertainty:** This is the most common thinking error in OCD. Because OCD is dichotomous (good vs. bad, black vs. white, right vs. wrong), you feel you must have 100 percent certainty regarding something in your life. The possibility of doubt or ambivalence feels intolerable.

2. **Intolerance of Anxiety:** You believe that the experience of anxiety, distress, disgust, or fear is never-ending and will not go away. This error is also tied to the fear that this experience will lead to a sense of losing control or other potential negative consequences.

3. **Emotional Reasoning:** Just because something feels a certain way, you conclude that it is that way. For example, if you feel anxious, then you assume that the food, the person, or the experience is dangerous.

4. **Need to Control Thoughts**: Because your thoughts feel so significant and meaningful, you worry that if you are unable to control them, something terrible would happen that you could have prevented. For example, you may feel that you would act on your unwanted thoughts if you don't try to neutralize them or you don't succeed in neutralizing them.

5. **Overestimation of Threat:** You feel that something is very likely and probable, when in actuality it is only possible. Negative outcomes then feel very likely or catastrophic. Remember that OCD confuses possibility and probability, making things that are possible seem like they are very probable and likely.

6. **Overestimation of Responsibility:** You believe that you are responsible for preventing harm from coming to yourself or others simply because you have thoughts about harmful outcomes. You perceive that failing to prevent or failing to try to prevent harm is as significant as causing harm itself.

7. **Thought-Action Fusion:** You believe your thoughts are overly significant, meaningful, and important. The possibility of something terrible happening feels more likely solely because you have thoughts about it. Also, you perceive the presence of unwanted thoughts as morally wrong and equivalent to engaging in horrible actions.

8. **The "Just Right" Error (Perfectionism):** You aim to perform certain tasks in order to achieve a "just right" or perfect feeling or a feeling of completeness. You do this to seek relief from tension or discomfort. You may also want to achieve symmetry or have things be evened out; you might also engage in magical thinking. This happens when you feel that if things are not done in just right ways, then this would cause a horrible, terrible, or unwanted outcome.

Activity: Many individuals experience these thinking errors. As you go through the following exercise, take a moment to check in with yourself and leave any judgment you may be feeling at the door. You are working to become your own expert and best ally. Understanding how your OCD works is a valuable part of your journey. Using the chart on the next page, identify a time when you experienced each of the following thinking errors.

Thinking Errors	Example
Intolerance for Uncertainty	
Intolerance of Anxiety	
Emotional Reasoning	
Need to Control Thoughts	
Overestimation of Threat	
Overestimation of Responsibility	
Thought-Action Fusion	
Perfectionism—"Just Right"	

How Thinking Errors Lead to Compulsions

The way you think influences how you feel, and the way you feel influences how you think, and both influence how you behave. Identifying your thinking errors helps you understand how this drives your OCD behaviors. You have learned that OCD behaviors are emotionally driven. Because the way you think is often reinforced by the way you feel, you tend to make behavioral choices based on thoughts that are tied to emotional experiences.

Experiencing distress often makes thoughts feel very real, and this may cause you to react accordingly. Your reaction or compulsion is often fueled by avoidance. You may want to avoid a potential negative outcome, an anxiety-provoking situation, uncertainty, or responsibility. By avoiding distressing experiences, you don't allow yourself the chance to learn new information about the experience and, in turn, you are not able to challenge a thinking error.

Reflection: How has avoidance reinforced one of your thinking errors? For example, you avoid eating a certain food you think is contaminated, and by avoiding it you confirm that the food is unsafe.

Reflection: What is one behavior that you can engage in that will challenge one of your thinking errors? For example, you have a thought that a certain food is contaminated and will cause you to become sick; however, you choose to eat it anyway despite having this thought.

Avoidance vs. Redirection

Avoidance includes turning away from, distracting from, or ignoring an experience. Avoidance takes away the opportunity to acknowledge and decide what to do about it. Awareness of when you want to avoid an experience is pivotal to changing your behavior. Pausing and acknowledging your desire to avoid gives you the opportunity to choose what you want to do next—move away or toward your values.

When you choose not to avoid and instead decide to *redirect* your behavior in a values-driven way, it allows you to learn, grow, and challenge your fears. Redirecting your behavior is about turning toward instead of away from fears. By identifying the intention behind a behavior, you can differentiate if this behavior is driven by avoidance or driven by values. A behavior fueled by the urge to avoid is one that is chosen due to fear, discomfort, uncertainty, or the idea of having an unpleasant experience. However, a behavior guided by your values is one that aligns with what you want in life, how you want to live, or what is important to you. It all comes down to your intention and how this affects your choices and behaviors.

Avoidance includes turning away from, distracting from, or ignoring something.
Redirecting your behavior is about turning toward instead of away from fears.

Identifying Your Intention Activity

- What are your go-to behaviors when you feel distress, fear, discomfort, or concern about experiencing something unpleasant?

  ____

  ____

  ____

- Does this choice align with your values? How can you tell?

  ____

  ____

  ____

- What is your intention? Are you trying to avoid an experience? Are you trying to reinforce something that is important to you?

  ____

  ____

  ____

Engaging in values-driven behaviors is a practice. It will take time to master this skill. Because we are human, we will never reach perfection. Keep in mind that values are a guiding light and not a goal or a finish line to reach. Have compassion for yourself if you find that choosing a values-driven behavior is too challenging and you choose avoidance instead. Use this opportunity as a learning experience by staying curious and open-minded about how this can help you grow and become your own expert and best ally.

In this moment, there is plenty of time. In this moment, you are precisely as you should be. In this moment, there is infinite possibility.

—Victoria Moran

Chapter 5

Challenging Diet Culture and Leaning into Discomfort

In chapter 2, you learned that diet culture is rooted in a black-and-white perspective. Diet culture states that if you adhere to its strict sets of rules and beliefs around food, eating, movement, and body shapes and sizes, you are "right," "successful," and "good." As human beings, many of us strive to do the right thing most of the time. Our tendency is to focus on what we feel is incorrect and needs fixing while often overlooking and ignoring the things that we feel don't need fixing.

Diet culture overemphasizes that there is something that needs fixing when it comes to your body, eating practices, and movement. When you have a diet culture mindset, you can feel like you are never doing enough.

Diet Culture and Perfectionism

Living in a diet culture world, you are constantly bombarded with messages around ideal thin bodies, restrictions, the perfect workout, the best diet, and the latest quick fix or cleanse. You may try to get away from these messages, but they are everywhere: from social media to food packaging to conversations with friends or family members.

As humans, when we are surrounded by an extreme amount of information that is difficult to integrate or make sense of, it is inevitable that this results in questioning ourselves, our perspectives, and our values. Because of this, we continuously feel that we are not getting it right and are making mistakes. In efforts to fix our mistakes, we can find ourselves going down the rabbit hole of information gathering, which ultimately increases our confusion. Because of diet culture's faulty framework, it's difficult to reach a satisfactory level of success or achievement. In diet culture, our efforts are never enough, and achievements are constantly redefined, similar to a moving target.

Diet culture does not honor your unique needs. It overlooks the individuality of each human being by making blanket statements around what is "good," "right," or "moral." Diet culture operates from a perfectionistic framework. *Perfectionism* is a trait often seen in OCD. Perfectionism is an unwillingness to accept anything less than the best. When you are perfectionistic, you strive to avoid mistakes and set unattainably high standards while engaging in harsh self-criticism.

Perfectionism is an unwillingness to accept anything less than the best. When you are perfectionistic, you strive to avoid mistakes and set unattainably high standards while engaging in harsh self-criticism.

Challenging perfectionism is a large component of your healing journey. And, in fact, making mistakes is a part of it rather than the exception. When you learn to challenge perfectionism, you learn how to challenge both OCD and diet culture.

Reflection: As you check in with yourself regarding how diet culture has influenced you, take a moment to remember that your environment has a large impact on how you think, feel, and behave. Because of this, you may not have even been aware of how your thoughts, feelings, and behaviors are tied to diet culture. Be kind to yourself as you complete reflection questions below.

In what ways has diet culture influenced the way you think, feel, or behave regarding the following:

- Your body shape and size

____

____

____

____

- Your overall health

____

____

____

____

- Your food/eating choices (e.g., types, amounts, location, companion(s))

- Your style of eating (e.g., vegetarian, vegan, ketogenic, macros, etc.)

- Your movement/exercise

- Another area of your life

Activity: Never-Ending Marathon

You learned how the desire to get things right fuels OCD, and this is often reflected in diet culture. When you have a diet culture mentality, you may find yourself exhausted trying to continuously reach that perfect point of achievement to no avail. Fortunately, there are alternatives.

Please take a moment to think about the effort and amount of time you are spending trying to reach perfection for certain behaviors, activities, or thoughts. Now, picture yourself at the starting line of a marathon. You have trained and feel prepared. The race starts and you begin running. You know where the finish line is and pace yourself accordingly. You feel strong and determined. You are running well and can see the finish line.

As you approach the finish line, you notice something puzzling. The finish line is no longer where you thought it would have been. To your surprise, the finish line is actually up ahead. You keep running, hoping to get closer to it, but you realize that the closer you think you are, the further away the finish line continues to be. You're feeling exhausted, depleted, and discouraged. However, you continue running because you feel that the only way that you can end the marathon is if you reach the finish line.

- What goals have felt like a never-ending marathon for you? For example, being thin enough, clean enough, healthy enough, safe enough, etc.?

____

____

____

- How might these efforts affect your life (e.g., relationships, food and eating choices, job/school, social life)? For instance, wanting to reach a certain weight before I wear a bathing suit and go to the beach or cleaning my house to a specific standard before I invite friends over.

____

____

____

- Is the amount of effort and time worth it? How might you feel when your effort is not producing the results you want?

____

____

____

Being aware of how perfectionism is affecting your life will enable you to make choices that align with you and your values and not your OCD. You can make a different choice and end the struggle and the race. Letting go of perfectionism and choosing acceptance of what is allows you to walk away and end the never-ending marathon.

Leaning into Discomfort

Up until now, you have most likely functioned along perfectionistic frameworks that exhaust you. The idea of getting something wrong or doing something not quite right might seem foreign and uncomfortable. Challenging OCD can look like not scratching an itchy mosquito bite. When you do scratch it, initially you experience relief, but in the long run the itch becomes more intense. However, when you acknowledge this discomfort and allow it to exist and not scratch it, the quicker you can move past it and refocus your attention on what truly matters to you. By leaning into this discomfort and accepting what is, you are letting go of the struggle, and as mentioned previously, you are choosing to quit the never-ending marathon.

One of the ways in which you can practice leaning into discomfort is by engaging in *imperfection risks*. Imperfection risks are instances where you intentionally choose to do something that feels wrong and challenge the idea that there is only one right way to do it. When you choose to lean into this discomfort on purpose, it will feel uncomfortable.

Imperfection risks are instances where you intentionally choose to do something that feels wrong and challenge the idea that there is only one right way to do it.

Diet Culture and Your Body

Imperfection risks around our bodies and the way we eat might be especially challenging to take due to the fear of judgment stemming from a diet culture mindset. Our culture stigmatizes larger bodies and "poor" eating habits while glorifying the thin ideal. This is due to *fat phobia*. Fat phobia is a social stigma and expression of harmful attitudes and behaviors that shames, discriminates, and is biased against people in larger bodies. This is also known as anti-fat bias or weight stigma.

Our culture is very uncomfortable around fatness and therefore, there is a significant aversion to it. Fat phobia is deeply rooted in the misguided idea that a thin body is the ultimate life goal, and living in a larger body represents a moral failing.

People living in larger bodies can experience fat phobia in various ways, such as experiencing an environment that is not made to fit their bodies, like an airplane seat or a waiting room chair at the doctor's office. Fat phobia is also experienced when individuals have challenges finding clothes that fit. Or when they experience negative comments from people in their lives or through social media about their bodies and assumptions about their health, lifestyle, and food choices. Additionally, fat phobia can be encountered as health prejudice, medical misconceptions, and judgments regarding correlations between body size and health. These experiences are very real and valid and rooted in a flawed perspective due to diet culture.

Folks in smaller bodies are also not free from experiencing fat phobia. Regardless of body size, we all live within the same diet culture environments. Individuals in smaller bodies succumb to the same types of fears and concerns, even though they may not experience the same prejudice as those in larger bodies. Just like those in larger bodies, people in smaller bodies may also avoid eating the "wrong" foods due to fearing that their bodies would change and their chances of experiencing weight stigma would increase.

Even though this is often not discussed, it is a common experience to criticize, compare, and engage in diet talk among individuals of all body shapes and sizes. Unfortunately, these behaviors have been reinforced and normalized as a way of creating connection for people.

When one person brings up something about their body they dislike, another person may verbalize experiencing the same dislike, thus creating commonality and connection. It is the individual that is more accepting of their body that tends to be the one left out of the conversation. Because the norm is to be critical, to be accepting of one's body can seem like a radical idea. To oppose this norm can be uncomfortable and challenging.

Diet Culture and Mindful Movement

How diet culture defines exercise and working out follows the black-and-white mentality. It is based on rules and rigidity. If we don't adhere to these rules, then we feel that we are not enough and we may even feel shame. Diet culture tells us that we should be choosing only acceptable activities at a particular intensity and for a certain length of time in order for it to count. For this reason, exercise is often associated with calorie and fat burning, losing weight, sweating, punishment, and even exhaustion.

Diet culture's goal is to achieve and then maintain a particular body shape and size. It is not about enjoyment or moving our bodies. This perspective overlooks other beneficial reasons for moving our bodies, which include stress relief, being outdoors, connecting with others, learning a new skill, and having fun.

Mindful movement refers to freedom from diet culture's rules in how you choose to move your body. It also includes freedom from OCD rules. Similar to intuitive eating, mindful movement encourages you to make decisions on how much or how little you choose to move your body based on your needs, wants, and inner and outer wisdom. This is a gentle approach that encompasses curiosity, awareness, and compassion and includes a wide variety of activities.

The purpose of movement in this approach takes the focus off of the intention to change your body shape and size. At the same time, it quiets OCD rules regarding when, what, how, and how much you're supposed to move your body.

Mindful movement encourages you to make decisions on how much or how little you choose to move your body based on your needs, wants, and inner and outer wisdom.

Reflection: At times, it might be difficult to tease apart what is driving your choices regarding movement. Diet culture, OCD, or mindfulness can be influencing the way you move. In what ways has OCD determined how you move your body? Some examples of this might be: having to run for a specific amount of time that feels just right, not allowing yourself to end your workout until a certain number of calories are burned, completing an even number of repetitions, or having to do particular exercises in a specific order.

____

____

____

____

____

____

Breaking the Rules of Diet Culture

Breaking the rules of diet culture can be an uncomfortable but worthwhile process. This involves being more accepting of our bodies, which can result in becoming an outlier and experiencing judgment from those who adhere to diet culture. Challenging these rules is a freeing process and will enable you to make choices regarding your body, food, and movement that align with your values rather than diet culture rules. It is a flexible rather than a rigid approach. It allows you to check in with yourself and make decisions based on what you like, want, and need. Making intuitive and mindful choices around food and eating is an intention of recovery that opposes diet culture. This is referred to as *food freedom*.

Food freedom is making intuitive and mindful choices around food and eating.

At first, it can feel like you are making mistakes when you veer away from the norms set by diet culture and instead choose food freedom. For this reason, consider how engaging in imperfection risks may allow you to challenge diet culture and realign with your own values while challenging OCD.

Reflection: Take a moment to think about the ways in which diet culture has forced you to make choices around your body, food, and movement. Be gentle with yourself as you think about these experiences. Many of these choices may have been reinforced and have now become second nature for you due to the culture that we live in. The next step may feel radical and intimidating. As you complete this reflection, please remember to tap into your values and willingness. In what ways might you engage in imperfection risks while challenging diet culture and OCD regarding the following:

- Your body shape and size

  ____

  ____

- Your overall health

  ____

  ____

- Your food/eating choices (e.g., types, amounts, location)

  ____

  ____

- Your style of eating (e.g., vegetarian, vegan, ketogenic, macros, etc.)

  ____

  ____

- Your movement/exercise

  ____

  ____

- Another area of your life

  ____

  ____

Making Intuitive, Mindful, and Values-Driven Food Choices

Food has often been overemphasized as a determinant of health and well-being. There tends to be huge amounts of pressure to eat just right or healthy. Pressure and rigidity reinforce one another and oppose food freedom. Food freedom is adopting an intuitive eating mindset and lifestyle, one in which you are living in a gray area rather than a black-and-white or an all-or-nothing mentality. Therefore, food freedom and recovery from OCD go hand in hand.

Activity: Living Life Fully Outside of Diet Culture

There is more to how we live life than the way we eat and the food we choose, despite what diet culture wants us to believe. Each individual defines what a fulfilled life means to them differently. You may recall from your values exercise in chapter 3 that certain values are very important to you while others are not. How you choose to live your life is an independent decision and unique to your own preferences, ideals, and values.

Take a moment to think about your life and what you value. Next, think about how you want to live your life if diet culture and OCD weren't in charge. As you think about this, stay curious and have compassion. What would you be doing? What would be important to you? Please rate the importance of the following possible components of living a fulfilled life from 0 (not important at all) to 5 (very important).

Possible Components of Living a Fulfilled Life	0	1	2	3	4	5
Connecting with others						
Caring for others (altruism)						
Having new experiences						
Moving your body in enjoyable ways						
Emotional awareness and growth						
Learning and growing						
Having enjoyable and/or peaceful eating/food experiences						
Having a connection with something greater than myself (spiritual)						
Engaging in purposeful or meaningful work/school						
Attaining and building a support network						

Possible Components of Living a Fulfilled Life	0	1	2	3	4	5
Having a comfortable and safe living environment						
Obtaining enough rest and relaxation						
Getting quality sleep						
Other:						
Other:						

Reflection: Now that you have rated the above components, pause to reflect on what intentions you may want to set that align with living a fulfilled life. What behavioral changes would you be willing to make to move in this direction? Remember the role of values, imperfection risks, and breaking diet culture rules in helping you achieve this.

____

____

____

____

____

____

How do these intentions differ from intentions driven by OCD and food and eating fears?

____

____

____

____

____

Please list some steps that you would be willing to take to move toward your intentions to live life fully.

___

___

___

___

___

___

___

___

Keep in mind that you get to define what being healthy and living a fulfilled life mean to you. It's impossible for diet culture to make blanket statements regarding every single person's dietary and physical activity needs. There is no universal approach for all. Diet culture and media tell you what a fulfilled life is supposed to look like, but in reality, you are the expert of what that means for you. Part of healing your relationship with food, body, and movement is having the power to choose and define the life you want to live.

Part 2

Skills—Building the Foundation to Challenge Your OCD Food and Eating Fears

"The ocean doesn't complain about the dance of ten million waves; so don't be concerned with the rise and fall of thoughts."

—Papaji

Chapter 6

ACT-Based Skills

Welcome to part 2! In part 1, you gained awareness of your OCD food and eating fears as well as your relationship with food and your body. You identified your values and learned to master how you think, feel, and behave. You also learned the role that diet culture and OCD play in how you choose to eat and move your body. Now, it's time for the skills-based portion of this workbook. Throughout part 2, you will learn skills to help you challenge your OCD and food and eating fears.

Acceptance and Commitment Therapy

Acceptance and commitment therapy (ACT) is an empirically based behavioral therapy in which values-based actions are the foundation for behavioral change. ACT focuses on developing awareness and being mindful of the present moment while increasing psychological flexibility.

The goal of ACT is not to eliminate challenging feelings, physical sensations, or thoughts, but instead the goal is to be present with and accepting of these experiences. ACT encourages committed action that is driven by your values and not the desire to avoid distress or unpleasant experiences. Taking committed action involves choosing to act based on your values (values-based) rather than moving away from your values (OCD-based) and the life you desire.

> The goal of ACT is not to eliminate challenging feelings, physical sensations, or thoughts, but instead the goal is to be present with and accepting of these experiences. ACT encourages committed action that is driven by your values and not the desire to avoid distress or unpleasant experiences. Taking committed action involves choosing to act based on your values rather than moving away from your values and the life you desire.

Present Moment

A significant component of an ACT approach to OCD is the ability to connect to the present moment with full awareness nonjudgmentally. Being mindful of your experiences means that you are able to observe them for what they are, without wishing they were different, or telling yourself that you "should" think, feel, or behave differently.

Guided Mindful Check-In

Please take this moment to check in with your current experience. Look at your surroundings and pay attention to your breath. Please name five things you can see, four things you can touch, three things you can hear, two things you can smell, and one thing you can taste.

Now, bring your attention to your body. What physical sensations are you experiencing? For instance, are you feeling warm, cold, or comfortable? Are you experiencing any pain? If yes, is it intense, throbbing, radiating, or dull? Are you able to feel your feet touching the ground or your socks or your shoes? How does the chair or couch feel on your back or legs? Are you noticing any pleasant sensations such as a soft blanket on your lap or sunlight on your face?

Finally, check in with your level of hunger or fullness. How hungry or full are you feeling? Are you experiencing any stomach sensations such as empty, neutral, comfortable, bloating, nausea, or tightness? What emotions are you noticing (e.g., calm, nervous, anxious, sad, frustrated, energized, hopeful)?

Reflection: When you became more aware of your present moment experience, what thoughts did you notice? We invite you to take this chance to lean into this experience with compassion, curiosity, openness, and flexibility. Remember that present moment awareness leaves judgment behind. Please list some of the thoughts that came up for you as you completed this check-in. Pay attention to any judgment that comes up when you write these thoughts down.

____

____

____

____

____

____

Values

As mentioned in chapter 3, values are your guiding force in your journey to challenge your OCD and food and eating fears. Your values are unique to you and how you want to live your life. Therefore, values are your compass for taking committed action (action based on your values).

Activity: The following decision road activity demonstrates choosing a path that involves behaviors that move you toward your values rather than choosing ones that move you away from your values and toward OCD.

Here is an example to help demonstrate how you would use the decision road as a guide to make a values-based decision rather than an OCD and fear-based decision.

Let's say you are trying to decide whether to join your friends for dinner tonight. You take a moment to check in and recognize that because one of your values is connection, you would like to go to dinner. However, you also recognize that this decision is anxiety provoking because of OCD fears regarding the possibility of food being contaminated at the restaurant. You consider your options and your values. You decide to accept the invitation and join your friends even though you are fearful of the outcome. This decision is a values-based decision and challenges OCD.

Now it's your turn. Please think of an experience when you were making a decision and recognized that OCD fears were present. What would be the values-based decision? What would be the OCD fear-based decision? What did you decide?

____

____

____

____

____

To help you navigate the nuances of OCD and remain in a gray perspective rather than a black-and-white mentality, it's important to remember that even when you try to make values-based decisions, this might be and feel imperfect. Being in the gray area means that you are not trying to do things just right or perfect and that you are open to the possibility of making mistakes. If you always try to make the perfect choice, then OCD wins.

Every decision is an opportunity to learn more about yourself and your OCD food and eating fears. It is embracing a growth mindset to see how your decisions and actions align with your values. This will not only help you challenge OCD but also help you find food freedom.

Acceptance of Thoughts vs. Resistance

Acceptance means that we allow something to be just as it is without wishing it was different. Acceptance is taking a neutral stance and not placing judgment on what is by labeling it as good or bad or saying it should be or shouldn't be happening. It simply means that we let go of fighting and resisting.

Acceptance means that we allow something to be just as it is without wishing it was different.

Accepting OCD thoughts is the ability to coexist with your thoughts, make room for these thoughts, and no longer fight against them. When you tell yourself not to think about something, ironically, you are already thinking about it. As you have learned, the more you resist a thought, the more it sticks around. When you accept your thoughts, you become an observer of them and you allow yourself to open up to and even embrace them. Being accepting of OCD thoughts is an extremely valuable tool in order to defeat OCD.

To illustrate this approach, review the following chart that demonstrates accepting versus resisting OCD thoughts.

Accepting OCD Thoughts	Resisting OCD Thoughts
Noticing your thoughts without getting hooked by them	Mental checking
Embracing all thoughts	Ruminating
Letting thoughts be as they are	Trying to push away or control thoughts
Taking a nonjudgmental stance toward thoughts	Judging thoughts as good or bad/ appropriate or inappropriate
Opening to any type of thought	Disliking thoughts
Not labeling thoughts as good or bad/ appropriate or inappropriate	Distracting yourself and trying to not notice thoughts
Offering yourself compassion for having many different types of thoughts	Wishing you didn't have particular thoughts
Recognizing that you have no control over your thoughts	Not wanting to feel the distress, anxiety, or disgust that occurs because of a thought
Noticing and naming an OCD thought	Using breathing and relaxation exercises to get rid of a thought and the experience that comes with it
Allowing thoughts to come and go	Blaming yourself or others for having certain thoughts

Reflection: Most people with OCD toggle between accepting and resisting thoughts. When you choose to challenge your OCD, the key is to connect with your values and accept the experience of having OCD thoughts. You want to be mindful of not pushing the thought away, distracting yourself from it, or avoiding it.

Utilizing the above behavioral examples, reflect on which patterns of acceptance and resistance you typically engage in. Be present in this moment and stay curious and compassionate as you answer the below questions.

Which of the above do you engage in?

Accepting OCD thoughts: ____

____

____

Resisting OCD thoughts: ____

____

____

Recall a time when you accepted your OCD thoughts. What made this challenging? Did you experience an urge to resist these thoughts?

____

____

____

____

____

How did accepting your OCD thoughts influence your ability to choose a values-based behavior?

____

____

____

____

____

____

Your Relationship with Your Thoughts—Cognitive Fusion vs. Defusion

Your relationship with your thoughts is a significant determinant of how you respond to your OCD. When you fuse with your OCD thoughts, they can feel very convincing and true. *Cognitive fusion* is when you feel very attached to your thoughts and the meaning you give them, and therefore, your thoughts dictate your behaviors and actions.

Let's recall when you learned about faulty alarm systems in chapter 1. What you perceive as dangerous is reinforced by the way you respond to it. For instance, when you run away from what you perceive as dangerous, you are confirming that it is in fact dangerous and deserving of such a response. Unfortunately, by doing so, you are fusing with your thoughts and reinforcing them.

Cognitive fusion is when you feel very attached to your thoughts and the meaning you give them, and, therefore, your thoughts dictate your behaviors and actions.

How you fuse with your thoughts can take different forms and is reinforced by your reaction to these thoughts. Let's take a moment to review how *reacting* versus *responding* to your thoughts dictate your behaviors and actions. A reaction is automatic. It is an instinctive emotional response to a particular stimulus, trigger, situation, or thought. On the contrary, when you respond to a particular stimulus or situation, you pause, gather information, and then choose how you would like to behave. Responding brings awareness to the situation and enables you to make a decision rather than automatically react. The examples below illustrate how being fused with your thoughts is reinforced by your reactions and vice versa.

Example 1:

- **Thought:** "I am uncertain if this food will cause an allergic reaction."
- **Reaction:** Because of this thought, I avoid eating the food.
- **Cognitive Fusion:** By avoiding the food, I confirm that this thought is true and the food is dangerous.

Example 2:

- **Thought:** "If I eat at that restaurant with my friends, I will get sick."
- **Reaction:** Because of this thought, I do not go out to eat with my friends.
- **Cognitive fusion:** By avoiding going out to eat, I confirm that this thought is true and eating at that restaurant is dangerous.

In order to let go of cognitive fusion and stop reinforcing OCD thoughts, the key is to take an observer perspective and distance yourself from your thoughts. The more you can see thoughts as thoughts, as any other function of your body (such as breathing or your heart beating), the less you will ask yourself if a thought is true or not. This leads to acknowledging that a thought is neutral and not something you can control.

Cognitive Defusion and Psychological Flexibility

When you have a more peaceful relationship with your thoughts and are more accepting of them versus resisting them, you have a greater chance of choosing a response that aligns with your values rather than your OCD. The opposite of cognitive fusion is *cognitive defusion*. Cognitive defusion is the ability to respond to thoughts with curiosity, openness, flexibility, and compassion.

In this way, you are cultivating psychological flexibility, which results in your thoughts no longer dictating your behaviors. This then increases your ability to not engage in compulsions. Instead, you see thoughts as thoughts and as something that you coexist with and are separate from yourself (you defuse from them).

Cognitive defusion is the ability to respond to thoughts with curiosity, openness, flexibility, and compassion.

Activity—Defusing from Thoughts

Now that you understand what defusion is, it's time for you to practice defusing from your thoughts. The below strategies are examples of how you can practice this method. The intention is to cultivate the ability to notice your thoughts and then choose not to engage in compulsions by experimenting with one or more of the following strategies. This takes practice. So, please be compassionate toward yourself if you find this to be challenging. With practice you will begin to master defusing from your thoughts and letting go of the struggle while not engaging in compulsions.

Try using one or more of the following strategies to let the OCD thought be there without pushing it away, distracting yourself, or avoiding it by engaging in compulsions:

1. **Noticing your OCD thoughts:** Below are two ways to help you notice your thoughts. Experiment to see which one works best for you.

    a. Acknowledge the thought(s); notice yourself having it. Name it. For example, *This is OCD.*

    b. Take these steps to create more space between you and your OCD thought. Practice filling in the blank with your thought. Each step further distances you from your thought. For example, "I am having the thought that I will get sick from eating this food."

    i. I am having the thought that ________________.

    ii. I am noticing that I am having the thought that ________________.

    iii. My mind is having the thought that ________________.

    iv. I am noticing that my mind is having the thought that ________________.

2. **Don't partake in the food fight:**

   Picture yourself in a school cafeteria eating with friends when a food fight suddenly breaks out. Food is flying everywhere, and some items are landing on you. You wish the food fight would end, and you find yourself throwing food to retaliate. You throw one more item hoping this will end the food fight. However, you notice that the more you throw food back, the more irritated and messier you become. You also realize that your participation is prolonging the food fight, which is the opposite of what you want. The more you throw food, the more you reinforce the food fight.

   Now, imagine that your OCD thoughts are the food items and throwing them is a compulsion. In order to stop the food fight, you have to decide not to partake in it. It might be uncomfortable at first, and you might feel messy or gross when you allow food to land on you without throwing it back. However, the less you throw food, the more the fight settles down. Not partaking in the food fight is, ironically, the answer to stop the struggle with your OCD thoughts and compulsions. The key is to let your OCD thoughts be there; choose not to engage in a compulsion and tolerate having this experience.

3. **Imagery:** Visual representations of your experiences with OCD thoughts may help you build a more peaceful relationship with them. Imagery is a figurative way of describing what it is like to notice yet not engage with your OCD thoughts. Here are a few examples to experiment with:

   a. Watch your thoughts as if they are clouds in the sky passing overhead.

   b. Visualize yourself sitting in a movie theater and watching your thoughts as a movie would play out on the screen.

   c. See your thoughts as leaves on a stream floating by.

   d. Picture your thoughts as if they are music on the radio in another room playing in the background.

4. **Humor:** For some individuals, bringing humor to their experience with their OCD thoughts can be beneficial because it provides a different perspective, lessens the meaning of the OCD thoughts, and enables them to choose to respond rather than react to them.

   You may want to experiment with bringing humor to the situation by:

   a. Singing the thoughts.

   b. Imagining a character like SpongeBob, Homer Simpson, Shrek, or a celebrity saying or singing the thoughts.

c. Picturing a miniature human or character sitting in the palm of your hand saying or singing your thoughts.

d. Joking or kidding around with the thoughts.

Reflection: Now that you have different strategies to defuse from your OCD thoughts, take a moment to consider which ones you would like to experiment with in the upcoming week. After you have tried one of these defusion strategies, return to this section and write down what you noticed when you practiced this strategy. This is a practice and will take time to master. Be gentle with yourself as you experiment with different strategies and offer yourself compassion for the experience you are having. You may even wish to thank your mind for having these OCD thoughts because this gives you many opportunities to practice defusion strategies.

Strategy One: ____

____

____

____

____

Strategy Two: ____

____

____

____

____

Self-as-Context

The ability to coexist with your thoughts, make room for these thoughts, and no longer fight against them decreases the chances that you will give into compulsions. Now that you have practiced how to defuse from your thoughts, it's time to take it a step further and practice observing your experience of having thoughts. We all have a narrative of who we are based on our own judgments of ourselves and our experiences. This is referred to as *self-as-content*.

On the other hand, *self-as-context* is the noticing self. It is the part of you that observes your own thoughts, feelings, and physical sensations while being aware that you are not them. The noticing or observing self is constant and does not change. This is a peaceful viewpoint or perspective where you notice or are aware of your own awareness: a place from which you can observe your thoughts, feelings, and physical sensations without getting entangled in them.

Self-as-context is the noticing self. It is the part of you that observes your own thoughts, feelings, and physical sensations while being aware that you are not them. The noticing or observing self is constant and does not change.

The ability to practice self-as-context enhances acceptance of your present moment experience. This also facilitates thought defusion, allowing you to give less meaning to your OCD thoughts. Practicing self-as-context also enhances flexible awareness and a less rigid view of the self.

Let's look at a metaphor that compares the observing self to a cooking skillet and your thoughts, feelings, and physical sensations to the ingredients that will be cooked. The skillet is constant; it doesn't change. The food that comes into contact with the skillet changes based on the time of day, the meal, the ingredients available, and the way it is cooked.

You can cook many different types of foods on this skillet and yet, the skillet remains the same. Some of these foods you may like, dislike, or find to be neutral. The food and skillet are not in battle with each other, they simply coexist. The skillet is simply there to support the cooking process. The skillet is the observing self—it is in contact with the food as it cooks but it is not part of the finished meal—while the food symbolizes your thoughts, feelings, and physical sensations that are constantly changing.

Activity: Use the following chart to practice self-as-context. Please recall different food and eating experiences that you have had recently. Some may have been positive and enjoyable and others more challenging. Practice being the observing self and notice what thoughts, feelings, and physical sensations you can recall. Remember the value of acceptance and taking a nonjudgmental stance in allowing you to practice being aware of your experience.

Experience	Thoughts	Feelings	Physical Sensations
Eating pizza with my friend at a restaurant.	Will the pepperoni make me sick?	Nervous, anxious, scared, enjoying friend's company	Tight chest, nauseous, dry mouth

Experience	Thoughts	Feelings	Physical Sensations

What was your experience with being aware of your observing self? How did being aware of your observing self bring greater openness and compassion for your overall food and eating experience?

____

____

____

Committed Action

Committed action is at the core of ACT. Committed action is acting in alignment with your values despite discomfort or obstacles associated with OCD thoughts. By creating goals that align with your unique values, you are then able to take effective actions to achieve them. Effective action is based on your ability to be present in the moment and observe your thoughts, feelings, and physical sensations nonjudgmentally.

Committed action is acting in alignment with your values despite discomfort or obstacles associated with OCD thoughts.

Activity: Engaging in committed action starts with creating a flexible and values-based plan. Please begin by identifying the values that you chose in chapter 3 that will help you challenge your OCD food and eating fears. Consider how you would like your relationship with food to be or what you would like to be doing despite your current food fears. Be compassionate with yourself as you answer the following questions. There is no right way of creating this plan, and there is no intention that is too small.

Values: ____

____

____

Next, consider an intention you can set that is shaped by your values. What intention would you be willing to work on over the next week?

____

____

What is one step you are willing to take toward this intention despite discomfort and obstacles associated with your OCD thoughts? What actions will make your life fuller?

____

____

Bringing It All Together

By focusing on developing awareness and being mindful of the present moment, you are able to increase your psychological flexibility. Walking your OCD journey might feel treacherous at times, but increasing acceptance and no longer resisting your thoughts, feelings, and physical sensations will make the journey less daunting.

Values are your guiding light throughout this journey, helping you make choices toward your goals despite discomfort, anxiety, or other obstacles you might face. Noticing your experiences from an observer's point of view allows you to be more aware of them. This leads to being gentler with yourself and allows you to have a more peaceful relationship with your OCD.

"Wherever we are, we can take a deep breath, feel our body, open our senses and step outside the endless stories of the mind."

—Jack Kornfield

Chapter 7

Mindfulness Practice and Interoceptive Awareness

Being an observer of your experiences is a crucial step in becoming your own expert of your OCD and food and eating fears. So far you have learned about the benefits of moving toward your experiences instead of away from them. You've learned how this leads to a more peaceful relationship with food and fewer OCD compulsions.

This chapter will review the role of mindfulness in OCD recovery and challenging food and eating fears. Throughout this chapter you will learn how you can use mindfulness to increase the awareness of your experiences without judgment. This will allow you to have more adaptive and effective responses to your experiences.

Mindfulness

Mindfulness is paying attention intentionally in the present moment without judgment. Mindfulness encompasses curiosity, enabling you to notice what is going on both internally (i.e., thoughts, feelings, and physical sensations) and externally (i.e., your surroundings and environment).

Mindfulness is paying attention intentionally in the present moment without judgment.

Being mindful means that you experience what is without trying to change it or wishing it was different. Through this process of awareness and curiosity, you foster a nonjudgmental perspective, simply observing things as they are. Mindfulness also enables you to anchor in the present moment without getting lost in thoughts about the past or trying to predict or control the future.

Cultivating mindfulness is a practice because you return to it again and again. This practice is not meant to be perfect. It is an approach to coexisting with the present moment while observing all the components that make up this experience. Mindfulness fosters acceptance of what is.

Although mindfulness seems simple, at times, it can be challenging. Being mindful requires patience and understanding that your mind will continually have thoughts, ideas and urges while your body will experience various physical sensations. Through mindfulness you will learn to accept them for what they are. The intention is not to get rid of, avoid or clear your mind of thoughts. Instead, it is to simply be aware of and notice what is happening without judgment as best as you can.

When your mind begins to think about the past or future, mindfulness enables you to notice that you are no longer experiencing the present moment. Having this awareness allows you to return to the present moment. This dance of moving away from and then returning to the present moment will occur many times. This happens because your mind is like a puppy that constantly wants to explore and run away. The intention of mindfulness is to gently bring your mind back to the present moment with curiosity and compassion.

Mindfulness and OCD

Consider the mechanism of your OCD. Your OCD is reinforced by how you respond to your experiences. Avoidance of an experience reinforces the fear-based meaning attached to this experience. As discussed in chapter 1, through an inhibitory learning approach to facing your fears, you can create a newly learned safety meaning to inhibit the fear-based meaning.

Mindfulness seeks to minimize avoidance by increasing awareness and fostering acceptance of everything that shows up within an experience. By practicing mindfulness, you can notice, be aware of, and stay curious about the present moment without judging it or attaching meaning to it.

When you experience anxiety, distress or disgust, your immediate reaction may be to avoid this experience or engage in a compulsion to neutralize it. Alternatively, you can choose to take a mindful stance to this experience and simply observe it as it is, without responding in any way.

Mindfulness enables you to become aware of your behaviors, creating a space or buffer where you are able to then decide whether they serve you or not. This awareness allows you to decide what is best for you based on how you want to live your life. This, in turn, helps to foster both self-compassion and self-care.

Mindfulness enables you to become aware of your behaviors, creating a space or buffer where you are able to then decide whether they serve you or not.

Mindfulness Practice

Now that you have learned what mindfulness is, the following activity will walk you through how to cultivate a mindfulness practice. While you practice mindfulness, your mind may wander. This is typical. As you do this practice more consistently, your ability to become aware of your experience will strengthen and it will become easier to focus on what is happening in the present moment.

Some days (times) will be easier than others based on the presence of stressors, anxiety, or how loud OCD is. Being aware of the reasons your mindfulness practice can fluctuate is one way of practicing mindfulness. Staying curious and being compassionate to yourself during these practices is important because change only happens in the presence of kindness.

Staying curious and being compassionate to yourself during these practices is important because change only happens in the presence of kindness.

It is also extremely important to note that the intention of these practices is *not* to feel calmer or less anxious. Rather, it is to learn to make space for and experience all of your emotions, physical sensations, and thoughts—from pleasant to unpleasant—instead of resisting or avoiding them. It is a bonus if you happen to feel less anxious or calmer. If your intention is based on changing how you feel, this takes you further from mindfulness into a space of judgment. This would have the same unfortunate effects as a compulsion such as intensifying unpleasant experiences, reinforcing a fear, and depleting tolerance.

Now it's time to practice! There are many different mindfulness practices to try. In the spirit of letting go of perfectionism, there is no one right way to practice mindfulness. This also means that the components of such a practice are not rigid or meant to be completed, like checking off a to-do list.

Throughout this practice, remember that your mind is bound to wander. You can always bring it back to something that is constant, like your heart beating, your breath, or sounds or objects in the room or environment. These present and constant stimuli are called *anchors*. Anchors are a useful mindfulness tool to remind you to return to your practice whenever your mind wanders away.

Below is an example of one mindfulness practice to experiment with. Stay curious and have compassion for yourself knowing that anytime you try a mindfulness practice, you are building your awareness muscle and taking care of yourself.

APPLE(S) Practice

- **A**wareness: Become aware of your experience and what is happening (thoughts: swirling, calm, intense, peaceful emotions: stress, anxiety, sadness, etc.; and physical sensations: pain, empty stomach, tight chest, openness, etc.).
    - Stay curious by asking yourself, what's going on in my body right now? Does it stay the same, increase or lessen? What image(s), if any, pop up when you notice your internal experiences in this moment?
    - Simple awareness: Noticing if you are seeing, smelling, tasting, feeling, etc. Example: If you notice that you are seeing a bird fly by, you would state to yourself, "Seeing."
    - Examples of more complex awareness: Describe what you're feeling, noticing, or thinking, such as burning in my chest, warmth in my feet, restlessness in my legs, relaxed shoulders, a thought of being bored and lonely, feeling very hungry, etc.
- **P**ractice being **P**resent: Be present with what is, allowing what is going on in this moment.
    - It can be helpful to state the following phrases to enable you to allow what is happening without pushing it away or trying to avoid it. "Ah, so this is what is happening," "It is what it is," or "So, this is how it is."
- **L**ean in: Lean into your thoughts, feelings, and/or physical sensations rather than pushing them away or doing something about them; let them simply be.
    - Make room for everything you are feeling, thinking, and sensing.
    - Staying curious and having compassion for what is present will help you lean in and welcome your present experience.
- **E**xperiment: Experiment with creating space between your thoughts, feelings, sensations, and yourself. This lets your brain and body know that it's just a thought or sensation. You don't have to believe it or act on it. Try stating the following:
    - My mind is having the thought that ________________. For example, "My mind is having the thought that I shouldn't be eating this."
    - My body is experiencing a sensation of ________________. For example, "My body is feeling a sensation of tightness in the chest."
    - My body is feeling an emotion of ________________. For example, "My body is feeling an emotion of nervousness and fear."

Bonus practice: Now that you have learned the APPLE steps, you may choose to deepen your practice by engaging in mindful self-care.

- Self-care: Now that you've taken the time to check in and bring awareness to your present experience, take this opportunity to engage in something kind and compassionate for yourself. Examples may include:
  - Asking yourself: What might I need in this moment?
  - Placing a hand on your chest (keep it still, rub or pat)
  - Speaking kind words to myself
  - Understanding and compassion toward myself
  - Getting cozy on the couch
  - Taking a warm shower or bath
  - Fueling and nourishing my body
  - Drinking a soothing beverage
  - Moving my body in an enjoyable way
  - Petting your pet
  - Journaling
  - Calling a friend or family member
  - Other?

Everyone's mindfulness practice will look different and will vary from day to day. The key is to find what works for you and become more familiar with the way you function. It is very valuable to make this practice your own while you give yourself grace and let go of any rules around it. There is no finish line to reach with this practice. It's about the journey.

Activity: Chocolate Meditation–Engaging Your Five Senses

The following mindfulness activity is a fun way to experience all your senses. This simple method of practicing mindfulness can be done anywhere, anytime, simply utilizing a bite-size piece of chocolate. You may also choose another food item of your liking. For example, food in a container or bag that is bite-size such as a peanut, raisin, fruit, candy, or a chip. For the purposes of this example, we will be referring to a wrapped piece of chocolate.

Once you have your chocolate, find a comfortable place to sit. Notice any thoughts, sensations, or feelings that are present as you get ready to start this activity. Try your best to stay open to what may surface, without judgment. You are simply noticing an experience, without trying to make it be different.

- **See:** The first step is to notice and see the chocolate as you hold it in your hand. Pay attention to the shape of it, the colors, and the design on the wrapper. Is the wrapper shiny or dull? Is the chocolate round, square, or irregularly shaped?

- **Touch:** Next, take a moment to experience how it feels in your hand. Is it rough? Bumpy? Smooth? Is it heavy or light? Is it cold or warm? Is it hard or soft?
- **Hear:** For this step, you will remove the wrapper from the chocolate. Pay attention to the sounds that you hear as you unwrap the chocolate. Can you hear it crinkle? Do you hear it tear? Does it make another sound? If you are able to break it, what sound do you hear?
- **Smell:** Next, notice what aroma you smell as you slowly bring the chocolate closer to your nose. Take a few deep breaths. Does it smell sweet, savory, or have very little aroma?
- **Taste:** Finally, place the chocolate on your tongue. Take a moment to hold it in your mouth before biting it. What are you able to taste? Is it sweet, savory, or bitter?
- **Bringing all your senses together:** After holding the chocolate on your tongue, do you notice it melting? How would you describe how it feels in your mouth: smooth, bumpy, rough, or another texture? Now, go ahead and chew the chocolate and pay attention to how your senses might heighten. Are you better able to sense the aroma or the texture of the chocolate?

Reflection: Once you have completed this activity, take a moment to reflect on your experience. If you've practiced eating chocolate or another food item in this way, how was this time different? Or what was different in this practice from how you typically eat?

____

____

____

____

____

____

____

What parts of this experience did you find enjoyable or satisfying? What might have been challenging about it?

How might you implement this mindfulness eating practice to other eating experiences?

Interoceptive Awareness and OCD

Interoceptive Awareness is the process of being aware of internal sensations in the body, interpreting these sensations, and then learning from this information. Examples of interceptive cues (e.g., physical sensations) include hunger, fullness, digestion, heart rate, respiration, body temperature, thirst, and bladder fullness. Your awareness of these cues can help you decide how to tend to your needs, such as drinking water when you're thirsty or eating when you're hungry. In turn, the way that you interpret physical sensations can greatly affect how you choose to behave.

Let's consider how your interpretation of physical sensations can affect your emotions. Can you recall the last time you went on a thrill ride, such as a rollercoaster? You may have liked it, or you might have answered this question with, "I've never wanted to go on a rollercoaster." Let's think about how your body might have felt if you were in line waiting to ride the rollercoaster, or if you decided to sit the ride out.

Most people experience heightened body cues such as a rapid heartbeat, shallow breathing, or sweaty palms, and if they go on the ride they often experience dizziness. People pay to go on these rides and experience all these sensations because they interpret them as exhilarating. On the other hand, individuals who choose not to ride want to avoid feeling these heightened body cues because they interpret them as dangerous and unwanted. Both groups of people can experience the same type of sensations while interpreting them in opposite ways. One group enjoys the thrill of the ride and the other group dislikes it.

When certain physical sensations are interpreted in catastrophic ways, you are likely to feel anxious or distressed. Let's consider the role of fear in how you interpret body cues. Fear can take otherwise neutral cues, such as a fast heartbeat, and have you interpret it as dangerous or the possibility that something is wrong. When you avoid the experience of certain body cues that you interpret as distressing, this is referred to as *interoceptive avoidance*.

Recall the discussion on faulty alarm systems and anxiety in chapter 1. Thoughts, feelings, and physical sensations influence one another in shaping your experience and reaction to a certain situation. When cognitive errors, distress (i.e., anxiety, fear, disgust) and interoceptive avoidance are present, you are more likely to interpret a neutral stimulus as an alarm to danger. A significant component of challenging your OCD is changing your relationship with your body cues. The intention is to increase your ability to experience otherwise avoided body cues, even though they might feel distressing.

Activity: Interoceptive Exposure

For the following activity, you will be engaging in *interceptive exposures*. Interoceptive exposures involve deliberately engaging in an experience that provokes various physical sensations in your body that you typically associate with anxiety, fear, or distress. By intentionally bringing about these sensations, you will have the opportunity to practice mindfulness and experience them in a neutral, nonjudgmental way instead of avoiding them or trying to escape them. Remember that mindfulness is present focused nonjudgmental awareness. Be gentle with yourself as you step into this practice. This activity is a learning opportunity for you and there is no one right way to do it.

Interoceptive exposures involve deliberately engaging in an experience that provokes various physical sensations in your body that you typically associate with anxiety, fear, or distress.

While you practice the following exercises, try to stay present and simply notice your experience. The key is to get familiar with the body cues that may show up without judging them in any way (i.e., making meaning of them). Often these cues have occurred during situations where you have felt scared, distressed, or worried and therefore, you have attributed negative meaning to these sensations. For example, when your heart beats faster because your body is digesting food, and you interpret this faster heartbeat as something wrong with your heart and you feel scared. Being scared, in turn, makes your heart beat even faster, continuing to fuel your worry.

For each of the below exposures, start by practicing for an amount of time that would be challenging and you are willing to tolerate. As you practice each exposure, you may gradually increase the amount of time you're able to do each one. The purpose is to eventually get better at tolerating these sensations. You may notice that over time, the experience of any and all of these sensations is no longer attached to something negative.

Choose a space where you can do the following exposures freely. Please use a stopwatch or timer to help you practice the following interoceptive exposures. Start your timer and begin the specific exposure, noticing how your body feels as you do this. Practice this for about thirty seconds or an amount of time you can tolerate. For each interoceptive exposure that you practice, jot down the amount of time you did it for and what physical sensations you noticed. If any thoughts come up during your practice, be sure to write these down as well.

- Running in place

  Time:______________________

  Physical Sensations:____

  Thoughts:____

  ____

- Spinning in circles

  Time:________________________

  Physical Sensations:________________________

  Thoughts:________________________

  ____

- Breathing through a narrow straw

  Time:________________________

  Physical Sensations:________________________

  Thoughts:________________________

  ____

- Jumping up and down

  Time:________________________

  Physical Sensations:________________________

  Thoughts:________________________

  ____

- Lying down and placing books on your stomach

  Time:________________________

  Physical Sensations:________________________

  Thoughts:________________________

  ____

The intention of interoceptive exposures is to bring about acceptance of physical sensations even when you might first interpret them as catastrophic, allowing yourself the opportunity to learn a new safety-meaning for these sensations. Remember that similar to mindfulness, this is a practice you return to again and again. As you practice, your ability to create a buffer or a space between your experience and your response strengthens. It is valuable to check in with yourself regarding how your body feels as you go through different interoceptive experiences in your life.

Reflection: What was it like to do this activity? As you face your fears and lean into discomfort, remember to make room for self-compassion and give yourself whatever time you may need to practice. How would you apply this to any distressful body cues that you might experience when eating?

____

____

____

____

____

____

____

____

____

Physical Sensations and the Experience of Eating

You just learned how physical sensations can be interpreted in various ways. What physical sensations do you notice when you think about a food that you are fearful of eating? Does your heart race or do your palms become sweaty, or do you experience tightness in your chest or a stomachache? These sensations are part of the *fight, flight, or freeze response*. You may have heard this term before. It is an evolutionary response that we all experience as human beings. This means there is a purpose to this response that serves us in one way or another.

Think about the Stone Age and prehistoric people. The individuals living in this time period often experienced disgust when they tasted a plant that was poisonous. It is likely that this sensation served the purpose of keeping them alive. In today's world, we are much less likely to run the risk of coming across an edible poisonous plant in our day-to-day life. However, when you experience food fears, something as safe as purchasing produce at the store can evoke a fight, flight, or freeze response.

When you experience these physical sensations, your body is in a restricted state rather than a relaxed, open one which is often referred to as *rest and digest mode*. Being in a restricted state occurs when you interpret the food or eating experience as dangerous rather than safe. Therefore, you are on guard and hypervigilant to your surroundings and body sensations.

In this situation, your body is getting ready to fight, flee, or freeze in the face of danger. Your body is doing its best to keep you safe by sending various physical sensations to prepare you against this perceived danger. You will most likely experience a rapid heartbeat, shallow breathing, and heightened senses during this fight, flight or freeze state. When this occurs, it is very challenging to consume food because your body is on guard rather than relaxed and calm.

It is much easier to consume food when you are in a rest and digest mode versus a fight, flight, or freeze state. When your body is relaxed, it is better able to digest food because blood is easily delivered to your stomach, where it is needed to process food. Whereas, when you are in the fight, flight, or freeze mode, the majority of your blood is being pumped to your heart and extremities to prepare you to face the perceived danger. Also, because your stomach muscles are less tense when you are relaxed, your body is better able to receive food and be ready to digest it.

On the contrary, when you feel anxious, your GI system contracts and gets tense, making it harder for food to move through your digestive track. Due to this automatic response, you will most likely experience a decrease in appetite, a reduction in your ability to taste, more difficulty swallowing, tightness in your throat and chest, nausea, or stomach upset.

Oftentimes, this response leads to increased food fears and food aversion. Being mindful of your fight, flight, or freeze response can help you face your food and eating fears and increase your food variety. As you increase your ability to tolerate various physical sensations, you will increase your ability and, often, your willingness to eat food that you fear and really want to eat again.

Reflection: Using mindfulness will enable you to become more aware of the physical sensations that occur when you decide to eat a feared food. Creating a more peaceful relationship with food also means being at greater peace with your eating experience. This means that by being mindful of how your body feels when you eat, you become less fearful of your body sensations and therefore, more accepting of them.

Consider the following questions as you reflect on your relationship with your eating experience.

- What physical sensations do you experience when you feel anxious, disgust, fearful, or nervous? Where do you feel these sensations? How intense are they? How do these physical sensations affect your appetite and willingness to eat certain foods?

____

____

____

____

- If you do choose to eat a feared food or engage in a feared eating experience (such as eating at a restaurant or a friend's house), how do you react? For instance, is your eating speed faster or slower than typical? Do you have to eat the food in a certain way or take specific sized bites? Do you feel the need to eat alone or with a specific individual or in a particular setting? How might your posture be affected? Do you eat standing, lying down, or sitting? Do you feel that you need to compensate for what you ate by moving your body in a certain way or by restricting foods or food amounts in the future?

____

____

____

____

____

____

By participating in the activities throughout this chapter, you are gaining greater wisdom and continuing on the path of becoming your own expert. As you may recall from chapter 2, wisdom is your own personal experience combined with your knowledge. Mindfulness enables you to listen to and honor both your inner and outer wisdom despite what OCD might be telling you. As you continue to practice facing your food and eating fears, be mindful by pausing and checking in with yourself so that you are better able to drop your compulsions and challenge OCD.

The best things in life are often waiting for you at the exit ramp of your comfort zone.

—Karen Salmansohn

Chapter 8

Keeping an Awareness Journal and Creating Food Exposures

This chapter will discuss the value of facing your food and eating fears and revisit concepts of ERP that you learned about in Chapter 1. In the previous chapters, we explored the importance of identifying your values in order to make self-supportive choices and take committed actions. You can utilize your values to guide you in making choices about what anxiety-provoking foods and eating related fears you will face.

Avoidance reinforces food and eating related fears. Food avoidance or restriction is similar to when you try to suppress a thought. The more you try to push a thought away, the more that thought comes back. When you try to stay away from certain foods, either by avoidance or restriction, you are more likely to think about the food, be concerned with what you eat, and/or experience overeating episodes of "safe" foods.

Activity: Let's try this out. What if we told you: "For the next 15 seconds do not think of a green avocado." Are you ready? Keep track of the next 15 seconds on your watch, phone or timer. Okay, how did you do? Were you able to not think about a green avocado? Most likely, this was very challenging. Because you told yourself not to think of an avocado, you started the 15 seconds already thinking about it. Truly, we are not as in charge of our thoughts as we think we are. Every day, we have thousands of thoughts that we have no to little control of. The more we try to control our thoughts, the "stickier" they become and the harder it is to get rid of them.

Cultivating Mindfulness with an Awareness Journal

Challenging your OCD involves allowing yourself to experience all thoughts, feelings, and physical sensations without judgment. Similarly, when you are working on improving your relationship with food, one of the first steps to healing includes reducing judgment of certain foods so you can increase the variety of foods that you consume. This is why mindfulness is a very valuable component of facing your OCD food and eating fears.

One of the key features of mindfulness is awareness. Having greater awareness when choosing, preparing, cooking, and enjoying your food will enable you to enhance your eating experience. When building an Awareness Journal, you can acknowledge and explore physical sensations, thoughts, feelings, and environments that influence your food choices.

Keeping an Awareness Journal will help you recognize what you are experiencing before, during, and after eating. Use this tool to gather information as a detective would collect data. Staying curious and open-minded will enable you to explore this information with a nonjudgmental perspective.

Curiosity is a catalyst to learning from a new experience. When you are curious, you are open to learning new information about a situation by making room to experience all different types of emotions. On the flipside, when you are feeling fearful, anxious, or distressed, you may want to disengage from a perceived threat and avoid this situation. When you do this, you are unwilling to reflect, make changes, or challenge yourself because you are trying hard to protect yourself from a perceived threat. Opening up to an experience by staying curious will allow you to gather information nonjudgmentally.

Throughout the day, take a moment to choose what meals or snacks you will reflect on and jot down what you notice during your eating experience. As you become aware of the following experiences regarding your food and eating, have compassion for yourself as you complete this activity.

Below are suggestions for what you can practice becoming aware of and staying curious about. Please fill in the blanks, starting with the time of day in which you consumed food. Below is an example that you can reference.

Eating Times	9:00 a.m.
Energy Level	Low
Mood/Feelings	Anxious/Joy
Physical Sensations	Tight chest, nauseous
Thoughts	Will this make me sick?
Cravings	Sweet
Hunger/Fullness Level before eating*	2: Very hungry
Location	Panera Bread Restaurant
Who am I eating with?	Friend
How am I eating?	Slow eating speed, not paying attention to taste
What?	Bagel with cream cheese & coffee with milk
How much?	¾ of bagel & all of coffee
Fullness level?*	5: Neutral
Response or reaction to thoughts/physical sensations/ cravings	Nervousness about getting sick. Questioning why I feel nauseous. Asking friends if the cream cheese tasted OK.
Enjoyment level (1-10, from least to most enjoyable)	4
Satisfaction level (1-10, from least to most satisfying)	2
If unsatisfied, what might have been missing from your meal/ snack?	Something sweet like jam, fruit, or juice. Nervous to add any of these even though I really like them.

* (Based on hunger/fullness scale from Chapter 2)

Eating Times	
Energy Level	
Mood/Feelings	
Physical Sensations	
Thoughts	
Cravings	
Hunger/Fullness Level before eating*	
Location	
Who am I eating with?	
How am I eating?	
What?	
How much?	
Fullness level?*	
Response or reaction to thoughts/physical sensations/ cravings	
Enjoyment level (1-10, from least to most enjoyable)	
Satisfaction level (1-10, from least to most satisfying)	
If unsatisfied, what might have been missing from your meal/ snack?	

* (Based on hunger/fullness scale from Chapter 2)

Eating Times	
Energy Level	
Mood/ Feelings	
Physical Sensations	
Thoughts	
Cravings	
Hunger/Fullness Level before eating*	
Location	
Who am I eating with?	
How am I eating?	
What?	
How much?	
Fullness level?*	
Response or reaction to thoughts/physical sensations/ cravings	
Enjoyment level (1-10, from least to most enjoyable)	
Satisfaction level (1-10, from least to most satisfying)	
If unsatisfied, what might have been missing from your meal/ snack?	

* (Based on hunger/fullness scale from Chapter 2)

Reflection: After completing a few entries in your Awareness Journal, take a moment to reflect on your experiences. For instance, you may wish to ask yourself, "Uh, I wonder why I ...?" What patterns do you notice? What feared foods did you encounter, eat, or avoid? When did you feel most satisfied? What were your wins?

____

____

____

Values-Driven Food Exposures

Building awareness around your eating experience can help you become more familiar with the role of distress in the choices you make around food and eating. Anxiety, fear, or disgust can change the experience of eating, making it stressful and no longer enjoyable. Pleasure in eating can decrease due to fears and concerns. You may often avoid activities that you enjoy due to fears such as attending a friend's birthday dinner, partaking in a holiday meal, or traveling. Choosing values-driven behaviors helps you challenge your OCD food and eating fears and leads to living a fuller life.

Let's revisit what Carlos experienced due to his OCD food fears. Carlos began avoiding slimy foods after choking on sushi as a young child. In his adult life, Carlos felt anxious about eating out with friends and loved ones. Due to his fear of slimy foods, he was highly concerned about the options available at the restaurant. Additionally, Carlos worried about having access to water at restaurants in case he choked.

Carlos felt frustrated and sad that he was no longer enjoying the restaurants his girlfriend liked to eat at because these places didn't feel "safe" to him. He recognized that this was causing tension in his relationship. Therefore, he decided to face his fears and engage in values-driven behaviors by going out to eat with his girlfriend.

Reflection: How have your food and eating fears gotten in the way of you engaging in values-driven behaviors? What have you missed out on because of your OCD food and eating fears? Take a moment to choose different experiences, scenarios, or events. What did you notice when OCD got in the way of you engaging in a committed action?

____

____

____

Reflection: If you were to engage in values-driven behaviors and committed actions, what would you regain in your life? What would be different?

____

____

____

____

Values and Willingness

You have now become more aware of how anxiety, fear, and disgust in OCD can get in the way of events, relationships, and other areas of your life that you value. Your OCD experience is unique to you. Therefore, only you can identify what changes you would like to make based upon what truly matters to you. Please recall the earlier discussion in chapter 1 on the differences between motivation and willingness. When you value something dearly, you will find it more worthwhile to take a risk regardless of your level of motivation.

In the earlier example, Carlos valued having a quality relationship with his girlfriend and challenged himself to participate in experiences he used to avoid. Therefore, Carlos decided to engage in a committed action and face his OCD food fears by eating foods that he really enjoyed despite his fear that he might choke. Carlos began to challenge himself to eat foods that felt less "safe" by pairing them with foods that felt "safe."

Carlos also practiced being intentional about leaving his water bottle behind when eating at a restaurant. He then tried small portions of more anxiety-provoking foods, such as lettuce and broccoli, which felt slimy to him. He was eventually able to make these foods part of his meals. Carlos was ecstatic when he was able to eat sushi with his girlfriend, which he hadn't done in years.

Reflection: What are some fears you might be willing to face regarding your food and eating experiences that will enable you to live according to your values?

____

____

____

____

Leaning Into Your Fears Versus White Knuckling

After completing the Awareness Journal activity, you are now more familiar with all the factors that play a role in your food choices and eating experiences. Some of these factors make it easier for you to eat, and some make it more challenging.

Refer back to your Compulsions Inventory in Chapter 1 to review compulsions that can get in your way of being successful in your exposure practice. Compulsions often provide temporary relief, but they prolong the distress associated with obsessions.

There may be times when you are apprehensive about your experiences, and you engage in avoidance of a certain anxiety-provoking situation or food. Apprehension or fear of an anxiety-provoking experience often leads to *white knuckling* or pushing through an exposure without truly leaning into the present moment and all of your feelings, thoughts, and physical sensations. When you do this, you are reinforcing that this experience is "dangerous" and should be avoided.

Avoidance takes away the opportunity to gain new information around a certain feared food or eating experience. By letting go of avoidance and leaning in, you might discover that the situation is not as scary or disgusting as you experienced it in your body or you thought it would be. In other words, the "lion" is really a "bunny"!

Safety behaviors are like "crutches" that you think you have to depend on in order to get through a distressing situation. These "crutches" often get in the way of you learning your true strengths. By letting go of safety behaviors, you can gain greater confidence in your own ability to face your OCD fears. Similarly, by letting go of reassurance seeking, you can regain trust in your inner and outer wisdom to be able to face a feared food.

Letting go of checking behaviors, including mental checking, allows you to be more present with your eating experience, increasing your chances of enjoying your food. This can also be the case when you let go of reviewing what you ate. Consequently, you are able to be more present in other aspects of your life. Leaning into "not knowing" can provide freedom from the idea that you must only eat foods that you feel are "safe."

When you face your OCD food and eating fears and are able to let go of compulsions and no longer white knuckle your way through them, you lessen your chances of getting in your own way and giving yourself mixed messages. Engaging in compulsions only confirms that these situations or foods are as scary or dangerous as they feel or you believe they are. The goal of exposure practice is to have a greater ability to face your OCD food and eating fears despite any distress you might feel, allowing you to learn new information about your experiences.

Reflection: Take a moment to review what you have learned so far in regards to how your compulsions get in your way.

What would it look like to white knuckle your way through a challenging experience? What would you typically do? How would you feel? Would you feel apprehensive, tense, or fearful? What physical sensations would you notice such as tension in your chest, or constriction in your body or nausea?

____

____

____

____

____

____

What committed action are you willing to take to fully participate in a food exposure without white knuckling or engaging in compulsions?

____

____

____

____

____

____

____

Exposure Practice in Action

You have now completed an Awareness Journal and learned how anxiety, fear, or disgust can affect your eating experiences. You also learned how tapping into your values and willingness enable you to engage in exposure work. You recognize the value of letting go of compulsions and white knuckling so you can lean into your OCD food and eating fears. It's time to bring together all the information you have gathered and create your own food exposures.

Let's take a look at the Exposure Hierarchy activity below. Exposure practice entails facing your thoughts, physical sensations, images, situations, objects, and any other stimuli that provoke anxiety, distress, disgust, or another adverse experience. Keep in mind the importance of response prevention (i.e., refraining from engaging in compulsions) when facing your OCD food and eating fears during your exposure practice. When you choose what exposure to do, it's important that you create one that is challenging and will allow you to grow and expand your food choices/amounts *and* not be so overwhelming that you feel you are unable to complete it.

Imagine going to the gym with the intention to lift weights. If you lifted a very light weight, chances are this wouldn't challenge you and you wouldn't get stronger. Similarly, if you lifted a very heavy weight as a beginner weightlifter, this might not be possible for you, or you might end up injuring yourself.

If you wanted to increase your strength and prevent injury, a better option would be choosing a moderate weight. This would allow you to complete the repetitions you want and increase your strength. This choice is more beneficial because you challenged yourself and were successful in accomplishing your intention. Similarly, during exposure work, it's important to find your sweet spot by choosing an exposure that is challenging and won't overwhelm you. This helps you gain confidence in your ability to face your OCD fears.

Exposure work is a practice and not an end result because it is something you return to again and again. As previously mentioned, values are an excellent way to guide your exposure work. In this framework, values shape your behaviors. This is similar to dedicating your time to learning how to play an instrument when becoming proficient in playing this instrument is very important to you. You want to return to your practice on a consistent basis so that you can strengthen your skill. The difficulty level of an exposure is not as important as how consistently you engage in the exposure.

Exposure Hierarchy

Example using Carlos's experience from above:

What OCD food or eating fear are you willing to face first? (1: first to 10: last)	Exposure	How difficult do you expect it to be? (10 being the most difficult)
1	Lettuce on a burger	3
2	Roasted red peppers in a chicken wrap	4
3	Not bring water bottle to dinner	5
4		
5		
6		
7	Boiled broccoli	8
8	Small portion of sautéed mushrooms	9
9		
10	Sushi	10

Using the example above as an inspiration, what OCD food and/or eating fears are you willing to face?

Use the food inventory in chapter 1 to help guide you in completing your Exposure Hierarchy. Think about the foods and/or eating experiences you avoid and those that you enjoy but are afraid to engage in. Consider your values when creating your hierarchy. This hierarchy is unique to you and what you want to work on. Have flexibility, be gentle with yourself, and stay curious.

What OCD food or eating fear are you willing to face first? (1: first to 10: last)	Exposure	How difficult do you expect it to be? (10 being the most difficult)
1		
2		
3		
4		
5		
6		
7		
8		
9		
10		

Getting Specific with Creating an Exposure

When it comes to strengthening a skill, individuals tend to do best when their plan is very specific and measurable. The following chart was created to help you formulate a plan to best support your efforts in your exposure practice. After you select an exposure you'd like to practice, use this chart to make it as specific as possible. This will enable you to consider all the factors that increase or decrease your chances of successfully completely this particular exposure practice. Keep in mind the compulsions you would typically engage in when going through such a situation and include them below.

If physically doing an exposure (i.e., in vivo) is too big of a step, beginning with an *imaginal exposure* can be the first step to take. An imaginal exposure is when you visualize yourself engaging in the feared situation using all of your senses. Be as specific as possible during the visualization. For instance, where are you? What are you feeling? What are your thoughts? What physical sensations are you experiencing? What are you smelling? How does it taste? What textures do you notice? What is the temperature of the food? Imaginal exposures help you gain confidence that you can do the in vivo exposure.

The following is an example of how Carlos created his first exposure in order to eventually eat sushi again. Each exposure step will build upon your experience in tackling the previous one. We encourage you to move on to the next exposure step when you become more confident in your ability to face a particular challenge. Some signs to let you know that you're ready for the next step may include feeling bored by the exposure, experiencing less apprehensiveness, increased willingness, familiarity with the experience, and/or finding more pleasure when eating the particular food.

Exposure Creation Chart (Example)

Exposure (What)	Carlos's Example: Pairing lettuce (challenging food) with a burger and bun ("safe" food).				
Compulsions	Avoiding certain foods and restaurants; asking friend if the food is safe, carrying water bottle, frequently checking a menu before going to the restaurant.				
	Steps (from easiest to most difficult)				
	1	2	3	4	5
Where	Home	Home	Home	At girlfriend's house	At restaurant
When	Lunch	Lunch	Dinner	Dinner	Dinner
How is it eaten	-With awareness -Sitting in an upright posture with feet on the ground	-Typical eating speed and bite size -With awareness -Sitting in an upright posture with feet on the ground	-Typical eating speed and bite size -With awareness -Sitting in an upright posture with feet on the ground	-With no water at meal	-Keeping the same pace as girlfriend
How much	1 leaf of lettuce	2 leaves of lettuce	3 leaves of lettuce	Lettuce portion served by girlfriend	Restaurant portion
With Whom	Parents	Sibling	Alone	Girlfriend	Girlfriend
How often	Monday 1x a day	Tuesday/Wednesday 1x a day	Thursday 1x a day	Friday 1x a day	Saturday 1x a day
What supports you	-Parents offering encouragement but not reassurance -Positive self-talk	-Enjoying time with sibling -Using senses to be in the present moment	-Confidence that this challenge was completed before -Playing favorite music	-Importance of relationships with girlfriend & her family -Using senses to be in the present moment	-Being with girlfriend -Fun environment

Now it's your turn to create your first exposure!

Exposure Creation Chart

Exposure (What)					
Compulsions					
	Steps (from easiest to most difficult)				
	1	2	3	4	5
Where					
When					
How is it eaten					
How much					
With Whom					
How often					
What supports you					

Reflection: After completing each exposure step, consider what feared consequences you expected to encounter. Select a few steps from above to reflect on and document your thoughts. Identify all the things you were worried about and fearful of. Did the outcome of your exposure match your expectation? How were you able to go through your exposure despite your fear?

____

____

____

____

____

____

____

____

____

Establishing Support While Building Accountability

This chapter has given you tools that you can use to navigate your own journey, at your own pace, by discovering how your values are connected to your exposure practice. Because everyone's story is different, everyone's journey and needs are unique. Doing exposure work can be challenging, and creating the support network that you need is highly valuable. It's important to recognize that the type of support that each individual needs is unique to them.

You are likely to benefit from support networks because support can take many forms, including talking to a friend, family member or therapist, a pet you take care of, or a loved one that encourages you. It can be very beneficial to have more than one individual to support you because everyone brings something different to the table, providing different types of support.

"Shame dies when stories are told in safe spaces" (Ann Voskamp). Think about those individuals in your life who are a safe space for you and supportive of you facing your OCD food and eating fears. You may find that you have individuals in your life who are closest to you and part of your inner circle. These are individuals whom you tend to open up to more and feel safest with because they have earned your trust and therefore, you're able to be vulnerable with them. Other individuals who provide more practical support are those who are part of your outer circle. These individuals are problem-solvers, solution-focused, and strategists with whom you can brainstorm challenges together. Take a moment to identify who is part of your "inner circle" and "outer circle" of support by filling in the graph below.

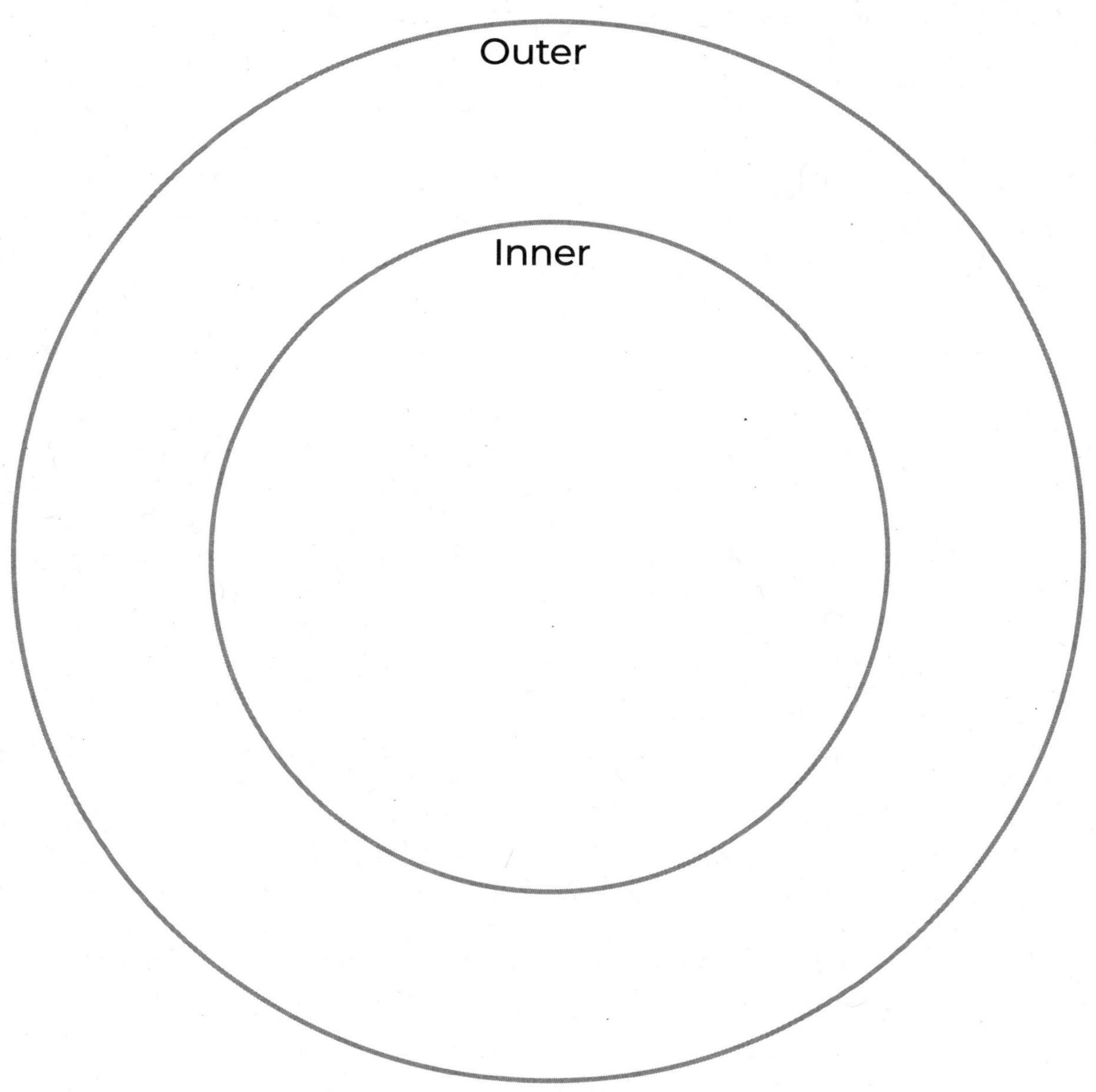

Reflection: If your best friend was facing their OCD food and eating fears and making a commitment to create a fuller, more vibrant life for themselves, what would you tell them? How might you express to them how you feel about what they are going through? What might they need at this moment? How can you best support them and their efforts?

Deciding what you would like your support network to be will help you identify who to turn to when the journey gets rough and who you might connect with to celebrate your wins. At the end of the day, the most important piece of the puzzle is you. Your biggest support is yourself. This brings the opportunity for you to be your biggest ally while you recognize the challenges of this journey. We can't tell you this will be easy, but we can tell you that it will be worth it. With this in mind, we encourage you to recognize how you are feeling and meet yourself where you are emotionally as you navigate the rest of this workbook. Review what you just wrote regarding how you would like to support a friend and apply it to yourself. In the next chapter, we will explore how to cultivate a self-compassion practice so that you can strengthen your ability to be your best ally.

"Self-compassion simply involves doing a U-turn and giving yourself the same compassion you'd naturally show a friend when you're struggling or feeling badly about yourself."

—Kristin Neff

Chapter 9

Self-Compassion

Completing this workbook provides you the opportunity to be your biggest ally. It will also enable you to better understand the challenges of your journey. In order to become your own expert and best align with your needs, it's important to meet yourself where you are.

The journey of facing your OCD food and eating fears is an ongoing journey of self-discovery and acceptance. Facing your food and eating fears is not an easy task. Everyone's fears look different and therefore, everyone's OCD journey is unique to them.

Self-compassion is essential for facing your OCD food and eating fears. Self-compassion is offering kindness to yourself in the midst of suffering or when facing a struggle. Being mindful and accepting where you are currently in your life allows you to foster self-compassion and let go of judgment regarding how your journey "should" unfold. The process of practicing self-compassion allows you to highlight and recognize, accept, and understand all of your experiences.

Self-compassion is offering kindness to yourself in the midst of suffering or when facing a struggle.

According to Dr. Kristin Neff, the pioneer researcher and teacher of self-compassion as well as the cofounder of The Center for Mindful Self-Compassion, there are three pillars of self-compassion: mindfulness, common humanity, and self-kindness (Neff 2011). Throughout this chapter you will learn about the components of self-compassion and how to implement this practice throughout your OCD food and eating fears journey.

Implementing Mindfulness and Reflecting on Your Experiences

The first pillar of self-compassion is mindfulness. Mindfulness allows you to be aware of your thoughts, emotions, and physical sensations without judgment. The practice of self-compassion involves becoming aware of your own suffering while having a nonjudgmental and curious stance.

As humans, we experience various emotions–some feel more intense than others. Our suffering refers to experiences of pain, turmoil, hardship, struggle, distress, or other unpleasant emotions. Suffering is a common experience of all humans.

Every individual experiences suffering in a different way, but this does not mean there is a right or wrong way to experience suffering. The key to self-compassion is to recognize that your suffering is valid, as is, even when others may experience a different emotional response to the same situation.

Using mindfulness enables you to be the observer of your suffering rather than giving too much meaning to your experience or, on the flip side, minimizing it. Taking an observer perspective creates a space between you and your suffering. This allows you to be with it rather than reacting in an emotion-driven way or attempting to avoid experiencing suffering. You cannot avoid suffering and engage in self-compassion at the same time. Through self-compassion you allow yourself to recognize and accept a tough or painful experience while, at the same time, not criticizing yourself for how you experience it.

You cannot avoid suffering and engage in self-compassion at the same time.

Reflection: At this point in the workbook, pause to recognize your progress. As you reflect on your experiences when facing your OCD food and eating fears, take a moment to identify a particular time when you experienced suffering. How might you implement self-compassion toward this situation? Are you able to acknowledge that this was tough or painful for you? Do you notice any urges to push away or judge what that experience was like?

___

___

___

___

___

Common Humanity

The second pillar of self-compassion is *common humanity*. Common humanity is the concept that all people are connected through shared experiences, emotions, wants, and needs. It encompasses a sense of community. In other words, you are not alone and isolated in your emotional experiences because all humans feel various emotions at different moments of their lives. Your experience of suffering connects you to others rather than isolates you from them since suffering is part of the *human condition*.

Common humanity is the concept that all people are connected through shared experiences, emotions, wants, and needs.

As humans, we are all subjected to the human condition. This means that we all face emotional challenges and are vulnerable, inadequate, and imperfect. Recognizing your common humanity will enable you to coexist with the experiences of suffering, imperfection, and uncertainty that all humans encounter. These experiences may feel very distressing, and you may think that there is something wrong with you. However, this is, in fact, what makes you human.

As humans, we are all subjected to the *human condition*. This means that we all face emotional challenges and are vulnerable, inadequate, and imperfect.

It is likely that throughout your life, you have been able to recognize when someone was going through a difficult time and provide them with compassion. At times, it may be easier to acknowledge and normalize the human condition in others while more difficult to provide yourself with this same level of understanding and compassion. This can be due to self-criticism, self-judgment, shame, and perfectionism.

Reflection: For the following reflection, take a moment to consider what it would be like to recognize the human condition in a friend or loved one who is facing their OCD food and eating fears. How would you offer compassion to this individual? What would you say to them? How would you say it? What might you do for them? How would you let them know you understand and recognize their humanity and suffering?

Self-Kindness

The third pillar of self-compassion is *self-kindness*. Self-kindness is the opposite of self-judgment. This is a mindful approach to recognizing your own being without judging who you are. When you engage in self-kindness you offer yourself support, comfort, and understanding rather than harshness and criticism when faced with a struggle.

By practicing self-kindness, you provide yourself with the ability to face your challenges and fears. This is because you approach your challenges with warmth, compassion, and gentleness. In other words, you can't shame yourself into change. Change only happens in the presence of kindness and compassion.

You can't shame yourself into change. Change only happens in the presence of kindness and compassion.

Imaginal Script: For this exercise, think of someone or something (i.e., a friend, loved one, pet, Buddha, character, etc.) that embodies compassion, kindness, understanding, and nonjudgment. Close your eyes and take a moment to envision how they look, what they are doing, and how they offer compassion to others. Write down their description below (i.e., name, relation to you, and their qualities).

What characteristics make them a compassionate being?

How do you feel when you envision them?

Now, think of a recent time when you were struggling or going through a challenge. How did you feel? What were you doing?

Next, bring your compassionate being into the space with you and imagine what they would say to you. How would they say it? How would they support you in your time of struggle? What is it like to accept their support and understanding? Do you notice any resistance to their kindness and compassion toward you?

____

____

____

____

____

Consider that you were the one imagining what this being was offering you. Notice that these kind words were coming from yourself all along. Inside you exists the ability to practice kindness and compassion toward yourself. At first, a kindness practice may be easier when you picture it coming from an external being. This can be a segue to cultivating the practice of self-kindness.

Backdraft

At times, self-compassion can be challenging. Throughout the above reflections and imaginal exercise, you might have noticed some resistance and distress when practicing self-compassion. *Backdraft* is the experience of distress, discomfort, and resistance that can arise during the practice of self-compassion.

Backdraft is the experience of distress, discomfort, and resistance that can arise through the practice of self-compassion.

Backdraft is often rooted in feelings of shame, guilt, and unworthiness. It exists when you feel that you are not deserving of kindness and compassion. It is a natural part of a self-compassion practice. Backdraft can help you identify cognitive errors to explore and then enable you to continue to move forward in your journey.

Utilizing CBT to Challenge Backdraft

Recall in chapter 4 when thinking errors were identified as unhelpful patterns of thinking. The way you think is often reinforced by how you feel. When you make behavioral choices, these are based on thoughts that are tied to emotional experiences.

An emotional experience of distress often makes thoughts feel very real and, therefore, you choose to behave accordingly. For example, if you feel distress when practicing self-compassion, you may think that you are not deserving of it and may avoid behaving in self-compassionate ways. Experiencing backdraft can make you more likely to avoid self-compassion, just like believing your thinking errors can make you more likely to avoid feared foods.

By avoiding distressing experiences, you don't allow yourself the chance to learn new information about the experience and, in turn, you are not able to challenge a thinking error or backdraft. For this reason, we approach backdraft in self-compassion similarly to how we approach thinking errors in OCD. We don't need to have 100 percent certainty that food is safe in order to try it, just as we don't need to believe that we deserve compassion and kindness in order to behave in compassionate and kind ways.

Reflection: Keep in mind that backdraft is a natural part of a self-compassion practice. Recall a time when you experienced backdraft. What thoughts did you have? What emotions were present? Did you notice any resistance to practicing self-compassion?

____

____

____

____

____

____

____

____

The first step in challenging backdraft is to acknowledge its existence. Recognize and label this experience for what it is without judging it. Name any emotions that might be present. You may want to utilize the APPLE(S) practice from chapter 7 at this time.

Ask yourself if your self-compassion intention is too grand and not yet attainable for you. This can often occur when practicing self-compassion. Rather than beat yourself up for not being where you want to be in your self-compassion practice, meet yourself where you currently are in this practice. Be gentle with yourself and determine the pace that works best for you. Meeting yourself where you're at will enable you to gradually strengthen your self-compassion practice.

Reflection: Consider how you may be able to continue practicing self-compassion when experiencing backdraft. Are you able to give yourself compassion in such a way that feels attainable? What might this look like? If you're currently not able to, what would you need to change in order to get there?

Are you able to recognize any thinking errors that arise when you consider taking a self-compassionate approach to your OCD, food and eating exposure practice?

What compassionate and kind behavior might you be willing to engage in despite any distressing thoughts and feelings?

Putting It All Into Practice

One of the benefits of participating in self-compassion is to strengthen your ability to lean into discomfort by diminishing self-criticism and judgment. In turn, self-compassion enhances your ability to engage in ERP while lessening avoidance.

You have learned about self-compassion and how you can apply it in your OCD journey. The following exercise can be used any time you are experiencing a struggle or distressful situation. This exercise provides a framework to help you cultivate self-compassion. It outlines how to practice mindfulness and self-kindness and recognize common humanity. You can follow the steps below as is, or you can change the order depending on where you would like to start.

The below phrases are examples of how you can acknowledge that you are going through a challenging time. You can utilize them to highlight and identify the components of self-compassion. Their purpose is not to make suffering go away, but to simply recognize it and accept it for what it is in a nonjudgmental way. You may want to create different ones that better resonate with you.

Mindfulness: Name or label what you are experiencing.

- This is a moment of suffering.
- This is a scary experience.
- This is a challenging moment.
- Other: ______________________________

Common Humanity: Recognize that as humans, we experience similar emotions throughout our lives, and we are not alone in our experiences of suffering.

- Suffering is a part of life.
- All humans go through challenging times.
- This is what it feels like to be a human who is struggling.
- Other: ______________________________

Self-kindness: Offer yourself support, comfort, and understanding in the face of a struggle. Consider how you will treat yourself or talk to yourself as a friend would.

- I am imperfect and that is okay.
- "Your name," I'm sorry you're going through a tough time.
- I am compassionate toward myself.
- I am able to identify what I need and provide that for myself.
- Other: ____

Reflection: A self-compassion practice is one you return to again and again. Over time, your ability to check in with yourself and offer yourself compassion will increase. There is no perfect way to do this practice. How might you be able to use self-compassion in your life? What areas might you want to focus on? What intentions will you set for your practice (e.g., stay curious, be nonjudgmental)?

Areas in your life where you will practice self-compassion. (For example when feeling scared to eat a particular food, going out to eat with friends, having to eat a nonpreferred or feared food.)

____

____

____

____

What will this practice look like? (For example: being mindful of whatever emotions show up, offering yourself extra time to move through a challenge, recognizing how difficult something can be, speaking to yourself with kindness.)

____

____

____

____

____

Pause and Check In

Pause to check in and see what you may need and want during this self-compassion practice. You may wish to place a hand on your chest. You may also wish to do something kind for yourself in this moment of suffering, such as choosing a values-driven behavior or a self-soothing behavior like going for a walk in nature, taking a bath, snuggling on the couch with a blanket, drinking a hot beverage, journaling, being creative, or taking a few deep breaths.

Remember to accept where you're at in your life and in your ability to engage in self-compassion. There is no right or wrong way to practice compassion toward yourself. This practice allows you to better engage in ERP and face your OCD food and eating fears.

Part 3:

Recovery: Living a Full Life

"Be gentle with yourself. You are a child of the universe no less than the trees and the stars; you have a right to be here."

—Max Ehrmann

Chapter 10

Self-Care, Support, and the Human Condition

Welcome to part 3 of this workbook. In part 2, you learned skills to help you face your OCD food and eating fears. You learned to not give into compulsions by aligning with your values. You practiced accepting your feelings and physical sensations while defusing or separating from your thoughts. You discovered how to implement mindfulness to build awareness of your food and eating fears. Using this information, you then created exposures. Part 2 also emphasized cultivating a self-compassion practice to better support yourself in your OCD food and eating fears journey.

Part 3 will offer you the tools to successfully navigate your OCD journey. Recall that change only happens in the presence of kindness and compassion. This chapter will reinforce this self-compassionate stance. The skills in this chapter will help you determine how to best engage in self-care and self-support.

The Human Condition and Eating Choices

Being human means that you are vulnerable, imperfect, and, like all humans, face emotional challenges. Facing your food and eating fears is not meant to be a perfect path, but one that recognizes your humanity. Recovery is not linear and varies from person to person.

How you challenge your OCD will also look different from day to day. Recall how recognizing your willingness increases your ability to engage in ERP. Although willingness is much steadier than motivation, it is also impacted by the human condition. In other words, when we suffer, we may still feel willing to engage in something challenging, yet our ability to do so might be compromised. Willingness might be affected when our level of tolerance is lower or bandwidth is smaller.

Imagine how you feel when you have a challenging work/school day, a fight with a friend, or a poor night's sleep. You are likely to feel groggy, low energy, irritable, or on edge. Chances are your levels of tolerance for additional stressors are lower, making it more difficult to engage in ERP. When your bandwidth is smaller, there is limited room for tolerating anything else.

It is important to meet yourself where you are and identify your level of tolerance. This enables you to decide what ERP you are willing to engage in. However, it will not be helpful for you to engage in avoidance. Be honest with yourself when you notice you want to or are participating in avoidance. Avoidance reinforces OCD and is contradictory to ERP.

When your tolerance is low, your willingness is impacted. Therefore, your ERP goal may seem too big, and you might shut down. Although you may want to avoid doing an exposure, rather than avoiding it, break down the exposure into smaller goals. By taking action even when you feel like you want to engage in avoidance, you are doing *the next best thing.* This is a powerful way to successfully challenge OCD while honoring where you are.

Doing the next best thing means choosing a more attainable goal and challenging yourself rather than avoiding or shutting down. This helps you realign with your values when your tolerance is low, you have urges to avoid, and/or your willingness is weakened. This practice increases your confidence and, therefore, overall willingness to engage in ERP.

Doing the next best thing means choosing a more attainable goal and challenging yourself rather than avoiding or shutting down.

What Does It Look Like to Do the Next Best Thing?

Your ability to tap into your willingness when challenging your eating and food choices varies day by day. This is based on how life circumstances influence your levels of willingness. To illustrate this point, recall the stories of Luke and Tasha from the introduction.

One of Tasha's values is to nurture her relationship with her wife. Additionally, she knows how much their date nights mean to both of them. Tasha had spoken to her wife about going to a new restaurant on Friday as an exposure. Friday evening, she noticed her tolerance for distress was lower and she felt irritable due to having a stressful workweek.

Although she felt the urge to avoid going out to eat, Tasha was able to do the next best thing. Tasha agreed to go out to eat, but instead of going to a new restaurant that was challenging for her, she asked her wife if they could go out to a restaurant they had eaten at before. Doing this allowed Tasha to challenge herself with the exposure of eating food that others prepared while also meeting herself where she was at by eating at a familiar place.

Luke's experience of doing the next best thing was similar to Tasha's. After performing poorly in a swim meet, Luke felt the need to restrict his food intake. However, he remembered his intentions around eating intuitively. He checked in with his hunger cues as well as his inner and outer wisdom and decided to make a sandwich. While making the sandwich, Luke kept experiencing a not-just-right feeling no matter how he built it. He noticed that he was becoming increasingly frustrated and defeated. Therefore, Luke wanted to give up and not eat the sandwich. Luke noticed himself at a crossroad; he could choose to restrict or do the next best thing. Although eating the sandwich was too big of an ERP goal at this moment, he was able to commit to eating each component of the sandwich separately.

Reflection: Recognizing your humanity in the process of ERP means that you meet yourself where you are and make a values-driven choice. What does doing the next best thing look like for you? Think of a time when your tolerance was low and your willingness was weakened. What ERP goal could have honored where you were in that moment?

____

____

____

____

____

____

Intuitive Eating Practice and Self-Care

In the above examples, Tasha and Luke engaged in self-compassion when they chose an attainable goal for themselves. They practiced checking in and making a self-supportive decision that aligned with their values. In this way, they moved forward in their OCD journey and prevented themselves from shutting down.

Intuitive eating is a practical way to engage in self-compassion. Recall from chapter 2 the ten principles of intuitive eating. Intuitive eating does not involve perfection or striving for an end goal. Rather, it is a practice that you return to again and again. Think back to when you first learned about intuitive eating and gained better awareness of your relationship with food and eating. The following activity will help you identify your progress in mastering your intuitive eating skills.

Activity: Using the chart below, consider how you have practiced utilizing intuitive eating principles to support your recovery. Reflect on your ability to do the next best thing and engage in values-driven choices that heal your relationship with food and stop reinforcing OCD.

Take a moment to think about your current food choices, eating experiences, ability to listen to your inner and outer wisdom, and how diet culture may influence your eating behaviors and food choices. How much do you agree with the following statements in the chart below? Be present and nonjudgmental as you check in with yourself and offer yourself kindness and compassion as you complete this assessment.

Statements	Strongly agree	Agree	Neutral	Disagree	Strongly Disagree
I do not follow diet culture's rules.					
I notice when I am hungry and eat at this time.					
I have a peaceful relationship with food.					
I reject rules regarding what, when, how, and how much to eat and choose what works best for me.					
I honor my fullness level and reach a level that works for me.					
I choose foods that I love to eat and are satisfying.					
I have different ways to cope with feelings and do not just rely on food.					
I provide my body with what it needs by treating it with respect and kindness.					
I engage in enjoyable movement.					
I rely on accurate and evidence-based nutrition knowledge to make food choices as needed.					

Reflection: Taking a self-compassionate approach to ERP helps you identify and choose self-care behaviors that support your OCD journey. Engaging in intuitive eating is a way of practicing self-compassion. After completing the above assessment, jot down examples of self-care behaviors that were guided by intuitive eating (e.g., *Making and eating lunch when I felt hungry rather than restricting. Attending my friend's birthday party and eating a slice of a cake they baked even though I felt scared.*)

____

____

____

____

____

____

Defining and Choosing Intentions

At times, it can be difficult to discern the reasons you might be engaging in a behavior or if this behavior aligns with self-care. It is possible that you may want to avoid discomfort and behave accordingly. On the other hand, when something matters to you, you may choose to tolerate the discomfort.

In order to distinguish if a behavior supports an OCD intention, it is helpful to determine if this behavior seems black or white, all or nothing, a success or failure, or is rigid. A recovery-oriented behavior is one that aligns with your values, allows for mistakes, is self-compassionate, and helps you live a fuller life and supports your recovery intentions.

In the chart below, take a moment to write down your recovery intentions versus your OCD intentions. Then, think about behaviors that you have recently engaged in and if these behaviors support your recovery intentions or OCD intentions.

Example:

Recovery Intentions	OCD Intentions
Engage in flexible eating Have quality time with my friends Try new foods	Decrease anxiety Get rid of uncertainty Receive reassurance Avoid feared situations

- What behaviors supported your recovery intentions?

  Visited my grandmother for dinner and ate the spaghetti she had made.

  Ate a few bites of ramen that I had not tried before.

  Let my friend pick the restaurant we would go to for lunch.

- What behaviors supported OCD intentions?

  Didn't eat meatballs at my grandmother's house because I was unsure what ingredients she had used and avoided this feared situation because I was afraid of getting sick.

  Canceled plans with my friends because I felt very anxious to eat food prepared at a restaurant.

  Ate the ramen at my friend's house that she had already tried because it felt safer and she gave me reassurance.

Now take a moment to consider and reflect on your experiences this past week. Using the chart below, write down a few of your recovery intentions versus OCD intentions that you can recall.

This past week:

Recovery Intentions	OCD Intentions

- What behaviors supported your recovery intentions?

____

____

____

____

- What behaviors supported OCD intentions?

____

____

____

____

____

Considering the insights you developed in reflecting on your past week, create some recovery intentions that you would like to set for yourself in the upcoming week. Also, think about what intentions OCD might typically set. Write both down using the chart below.

For this upcoming week:

Recovery Intentions	OCD Intentions

- What behaviors supported your recovery intentions?

  ____

  ____

  ____

  ____

- What behaviors supported OCD intentions?

  ____

  ____

  ____

  ____

  ____

Reflection: Now that you have practiced identifying and separating your recovery intentions from OCD intentions, consider and jot down how intuitive eating has increased your ability to follow the intentions that support you and not your OCD (e.g., *I listened to my hunger level and energy needs and chose to eat rather than avoiding food I wasn't sure was free of bugs. I chose to eat my favorite pizza versus what OCD said was safe to eat. I had breakfast even though I woke up feeling anxious.*)

____

____

____

____

____

____

____

____

Finding Support in Your Community

Self-compassion enables you to recognize and be aware of your suffering as a human. As humans, we all suffer at certain times in our lives. Being aware of your suffering will enable you to pause to decide how best to take care of yourself in challenging times. Reaching out to others for support is a pivotal and beneficial component for many during their recovery journey. You are not alone in your journey, or in your need for *community*.

Having a community means that you have a shared space with others who have similar lived experiences or who are understanding of them. Members of a community share similar identities, values, outlooks, and/or interests. Within a community there is a sense of belonging, respect for each other, and support for one another. Communities can be defined by location, age, race, ethnicity, interests, occupation, common bonds, and religion or spirituality. The members of a community encompass a wide range of individuals, including family, friends, coworkers, peers, healthcare providers, support group participants, individuals living in your neighborhood, and others.

Reflection: Creating a community for yourself is a very unique and personal experience. Some people prefer to take the approach of "the more the merrier," while others prefer to have a few very close individuals in their community. You may already know who the members of your community are. Also, you may now feel inspired to redefine or expand your community.

- Consider the communities that have been (or you think would be) an essential part of your OCD food and eating recovery journey. Write these communities down in the space below.

  ____

  ____

  ____

  ____

  ____

- Now, list the members of each of your communities from above. You might find that some members are a part of more than one of your communities.

  ____

  ____

  ____

  ____

  ____

- From these communities, who are one or two people that you can reach out to next time you need support?

  ____

  ____

  ____

  ____

  ____

  ____

Putting It All Together

Reflecting on your journey thus far can bring some insight into who you typically turn to for support. Support begins with you as your best ally. Meeting yourself where you are allows you the opportunity to make mistakes without shutting down. The key to navigating your recovery journey is to allow yourself flexibility while providing yourself compassion and self-care. The way in which you challenge your OCD food and eating fears will look different from day to day, and that is okay. There is no perfect path or right way of moving forward.

Doing the next best thing may also involve asking others for support. Although you may be your best ally, it is also extremely valuable to have others who can support you. It's important to share both your struggles and wins with your support network. Asking for and receiving support from your community will provide you with the care that you deserve, want, and may need at certain times throughout your journey.

And the day came when the risk to remain tight in a bud was more painful than the risk it took to blossom.

—Anaïs Nin

Chapter 11

Living a Full Life

Although this is the final chapter of the workbook, your recovery journey does not need to end here. Throughout your life you will continue to grow and strengthen the skills you have learned in this workbook. Your OCD food and eating fears journey will have ups and downs because you are ultimately human. The human condition is a lifelong experience of imperfections, mistakes, and lessons learned. You can always return to self-compassion and self-care to support yourself throughout this lifelong experience.

Recovery is possible, and each step you take forward is just as meaningful as the last. Throughout this workbook, you have learned to form a more peaceful relationship with OCD, food, eating, and your body. Recovery doesn't mean that you will never experience anxiety, fear, disgust, or distress again. Recovery means living a full life, on your terms, in which OCD food and eating fears do not get in the way of living your values or doing what you love. In this chapter, you will define what recovery and living a full life looks like for you.

Recovery means living a full life, on your terms, in which OCD and food and eating fears do not get in the way of living your values or doing what you love.

Finding Strength in Your Recovery

The function of recovery is to increase your ability to overcome challenging situations rather than prevent them. On the flipside, the function of OCD is an attempt to prevent undesirable and feared outcomes. This takes away your ability to learn new information about these situations.

An OCD cycle consists of behaviors that are driven by efforts to avoid anxiety and other distressing feelings and therefore does not allow room for self-care, self-compassion, or the ability to experience all types of feelings. Awareness of these behaviors will allow you the ability to get "unstuck" by noticing when you are caught in an OCD cycle.

Although this may not be easy every day, finding the willingness to engage in an ERP practice by meeting yourself where you are at is a marker of redefining your relationship with food and your body. Meeting yourself where you are means that you choose to do the next best thing when something is too challenging in that moment. By engaging in ERP, you are demonstrating to yourself that you can lean into and experience feared situations. This will increase your overall confidence during your recovery journey.

Doing the next best thing is a great example of being flexible while also being recovery focused. When times are more challenging, it increases your chances to do the next best thing by asking for and receiving support from others who are part of your support network.

The function of recovery is to increase your ability to overcome challenging situations rather than prevent them. On the flipside, the function of OCD is an attempt to prevent undesirable and feared outcomes.

Reflection: Consider your newly attained ability to increase flexibility, mindfulness, acceptance of imperfections, and tolerance for uncertainty. How would you define your recovery? How would your food choices and eating behaviors be different? What would your life look like? What would you be doing?

____

____

____

____

Recovery and Intuitive Eating

Redefining your relationship with food is an essential part of recovery. A peaceful relationship with food includes having flexibility; finding satisfaction and enjoyment around food is unique to each individual. It involves allowing yourself to eat the foods you enjoy and accepting imperfect choices, despite fear, disgust, and anxiety. This relationship is also based on your values and willingness.

In order to redefine what you want your relationship with food to look like, it is useful to consider what you are willing to let go of. For instance, compulsions around the timing of meals and snacks, food preparation, cooking and cleaning habits, clothing, movement, and exercise, and comparing yourself to others regarding food choices and amounts.

Recovery involves making intuitive eating choices around food and eating that are tied to and informed by your inner and outer wisdom. Practicing mindfulness around food and eating enables you to follow your inner wisdom, including listening and honoring your hunger and fullness cues. It also involves listening to your outer wisdom by using past eating experiences rather than relying on external rules and beliefs or OCD.

When intuitive eating is challenging for you, it is key to engage in self-kindness, as this increases your ability to make better intuitive eating choices. Through self-kindness you can acknowledge the challenges you may be facing while letting go of any judgment that may show up. When you do this, you are being kind to your body by providing it with what it needs and wants.

Activity: The following are signs that you are developing a more peaceful relationship with OCD, food, eating, and your body. These signs can help you consider how you define your recovery. How much do you agree with the following statements in the following chart? Remember to be present and nonjudgmental as you check in with yourself and offer yourself kindness and compassion as you complete this assessment.

Statements	Most Often	Often	Sometimes	Rarely	Almost Never
Not engaging in comparisons between myself and others.					
Challenging behaviors that keep me "stuck" in an OCD and food and eating fear cycle.					
Feeling ALL my emotions and responding rather than reacting more often.					
Practicing self-care in various areas of my life.					
Practicing self-compassion when I am struggling.					
Allowing myself to eat foods I enjoy.					
Being kind to my body.					
Increased willingness to engage in ERP.					
Doing the next best thing versus avoiding something.					
Asking and receiving support from others.					

Reflection: Based on the above statements, consider how you define your recovery. How would you describe your current relationship with OCD food and eating fears as well as your body?

____

____

____

____

____

____

____

Relapse Prevention

Relapse prevention is an essential component of your recovery journey. It will enable you to recognize and be aware of times you are moving away from values-based behaviors and instead aligning with OCD rules and fears. Relapse prevention includes recognizing your wins, slip ups, setbacks, and side quests, as well as how you can reach out for support when it would be beneficial for you.

Recognizing Your Wins

As humans we are fixers by nature. In other words, we have a drive to want to fix or solve what we feel is wrong. We also tend to overlook what is right or "doesn't need fixing or solving." The challenge in doing so is that we often miss many valuable pieces of information that can be useful throughout the recovery process.

In order to evaluate your OCD food and eating recovery journey more accurately, it's important to consider a full perspective that includes all types of information, not just what you think needs fixing. Recognizing your wins enables you to take a full perspective. This means acknowledging when you did something new or in a different way, decreased avoidance, challenged an OCD thought, redirected your behavior away from a compulsion, or faced a fear.

Reflection: Recall the past week and what wins you had. These may not come to you very easily. However, the function of this exercise is to encourage you to take a full perspective that includes all types of information regarding your recovery. Use the spaces below to write down your wins.

Now, think about how these wins tie into your values. Values are unique to you and how you want to behave as a human being and define how you want to act on a continuous basis. Consider if the behaviors you engaged in were driven by what matters to you, what you desire, and if they align with your sense of self (e.g., inner and outer wisdom).

You may want to continue engaging in this practice moving forward. Some people find it helpful to keep a "wins" journal as part of their relapse prevention toolbox.

Awareness of Slips, Setbacks, and Side Quests

Slips and setbacks are a typical part of a recovery journey and living a full life and not the exception. Some may call these side quests. Your awareness of these will ultimately bring you back to your recovery path. The important piece is that you utilize the information learned through these slips, setbacks, and side quests to help you make more informed choices moving forward.

In order to return to your recovery path, the first step is to have awareness that a slip is occurring. *Slip-signals* are indicators that slips are taking place. Being aware of a slip-signal allows you the opportunity to make a pro-recovery and values-driven choice as soon as you notice it happening. Examples of slip-signals may include skipping a meal or snack, eating a particular food many times in the same day, staying in when you wanted to go out to dinner, washing your hands more than usual when you are preparing a meal, or spending more time reading labels when you did your weekly grocery shopping.

Slips and setbacks are a typical part of a recovery journey and living a full life and not the exception. Being aware of a slip-signal allows you the opportunity to make a pro-recovery choice as soon as you notice it happening.

Reflection: Consider what you have learned about your recovery journey thus far, and what behaviors get in the way of moving forward in this journey. Please take a moment to write down the slip-signals that might indicate you are engaging in a behavior that supports OCD and not your recovery.

____

____

____

____

____

____

Reaching Out for Support

Chapter 10 discussed the importance and value of having a support network to lean on throughout your OCD food and eating fears journey. When the journey gets tough, remember the individuals you identified as members of each of your support communities. It is more than likely that each of these individuals will provide different types of support. One individual may not be able to provide all the support you may need. In fact, having various people to reach out to increases your chances of getting the full support that you need.

Reflection: How might you be able to reach out to the individuals in your support network in times of struggle? Do you find it best to reach out in a moment of struggle or let them know when you are about to face a challenge and could use their support? How would you prefer to communicate with your support person? Do you prefer face-to-face, a phone call, a text message, an email, or another type of communication?

____

____

____

____

____

____

____

Now that you understand the components that comprise your relapse prevention toolkit, you can begin to put them into practice. Each step that you take in relapse prevention will strengthen your recovery and your skills to challenge OCD.

Living Life to Its Fullest

Checking in with yourself and where you are at are essential components of ensuring a successful recovery journey. In chapter 1, you had the opportunity to check in and consider the different areas of your life to which you dedicate your time, energy, and emotion. These areas might have included social time, exercise, studying, working, sleeping, hobbies, etc. In this previous activity, each area or "pie slice" within the circle allowed you to acknowledge how you showed up in your life. This enabled you to gain a greater understanding of how you want to live your life.

Activity: Now it's time to reflect on what changes you might have been able to create for yourself and the life you want to live. Visualize the amount of time, energy, and emotion you are currently devoting to various areas of your life. Utilizing the circle below, create a pie chart to represent each of these areas. Take some time to highlight all of your wins no matter how large or small they may seem to you. Any win is an accomplishment! Allow yourself to be creative and kind to yourself as you complete this activity.

Reflection: Take a moment to compare and contrast the life pie you created in chapter 1 with this pie chart. Do you notice any differences between them? What is the same? Leave judgment aside and take an observer's perspective as you reflect on the changes that may or may not have happened. If you notice any judgmental or critical thoughts arise, practice self-compassion. You may want to engage in the APPLE(S) practice to help you stay present focused.

____

____

____

____

Reflection: If you noticed any differences between the two life pie activities, what might have helped you make these changes? How has self-compassion, willingness, acceptance, mindfulness, and intuitive eating helped you in this process? Offer yourself kindness as you reflect back and notice the changes you might have made during your OCD food and eating fears journey.

____

____

____

____

Reflection: What areas do you still want to continue to work on? How might you continue to work on these areas? Remember that your recovery journey does not need to end here. This is simply a checkpoint to help you continue to grow and strengthen the skills you have learned as this workbook comes to an end.

____

____

____

____

Reflection: Looking back, in what ways might you practice gratitude for the work you have accomplished and the wins you have achieved while completing this workbook?

Wrapping It Up for Now

Living a full life means living on your terms defined by what you consider to be peaceful, fulfilling, and rewarding. The rules and rigidities that might have kept you stuck take up less and less space in your life as you move toward your recovery. Achieving a peaceful relationship between food, eating, and your body allows you to have more freedom and flexibility in your life.

As you continue to engage in ERP, your confidence to confront and challenge feared situations will continue to grow and strengthen. You can always return to self-compassion, mindfulness, acceptance, and willingness. Every time you return to these practices, you build greater strength and learn new information about yourself and how best to continue your recovery journey. Even after you put this workbook down, these skills will stay with you. You chose to read this workbook, engage in its activities, and give yourself this chance and opportunity for recovery.

Even though recovery is not always easy, it is a worthwhile endeavor. You are bound to face challenges, slips, and harder times. These are all part of the journey and not the exception. You never start from scratch even after a setback because you're always learning and evolving. Using your relapse toolkit will enable you to recognize when slips are occurring so you can return to your recovery path and realign with your values. Your values will always be your guiding light and North Star. May you follow your recovery path with courage, confidence, compassion, and self-kindness as you continue to face your OCD food and eating fears.

Resources

OCD Resources Websites

- The International OCD Foundation (IOCDF)
  https://iocdf.org/
- IOCDF's Special Interest Group for OCD and Eating Disorders
  https://iocdf.org/special-interest-groups/eating-disorders/
- Anxiety in Athletes
  https://anxietyinathletes.org/
- Anxiety in the Classroom
  https://anxietyintheclassroom.org/
- Made of Millions
  https://www.madeofmillions.com/
- Peace of Mind
  https://peaceofmind.com

Eating Disorder Resources Websites

- National Alliance for Eating Disorders
  https://www.allianceforeatingdisorders.com/
- Southern Smash
  https://mccalldempsey.com/category/southern-smash/

- Health at Every Size
  https://www.sizediversityandhealth.org/
- Health at Every Size Community
  https://haescommunity.com/
  https://haeshealthsheets.com/the-health-sheet-library/
  http://www.healthnotdiets.com/
- ANAD: National Association of Anorexia Nervosa and Associated Disorders
  https://anad.org/

Support Groups

- IOCDF support groups directory
  https://iocdf.org/ocd-finding-help/supportgroups/
- National Alliance for Eating Disorders
  https://www.allianceforeatingdisorders.com/groups/

Find a Therapist or Registered Dietitian

- Tips on how to find the right therapist to treat OCD
  https://iocdf.org/ocd-finding-help/how-to-find-the-right-therapist/
- ADAA: Anxiety and Depression Association of America
  https://findyourtherapist.adaa.org/
- National Alliance for Eating Disorders, find a therapist: referrals@allianceforeatingdisorders.com or call 866-662-1235 or go to http://www.FindEDhelp.com or the FindEDhelp app. If you are in crisis or need immediate help, please text "ALLIANCE" to 741741 for free, 24/7 support. Helpline is open every M–F 9 a.m.–7 p.m
- ANAD: National Association of Anorexia Nervosa and Associated Disorders Directory
  https://anad.org/get-help/treatment-directory/
- EDRD Pro Eating Disorder Clinician Directory
  https://edrdpro.com/eating-disorder-dietitian-directory/

Podcasts

- Anxiety Society Podcast with Dr. Elizabeth McIngvale and Cali Werner
  https://www.anxietysocietypodcast.com/
- The OCD Stories hosted by Stuart Ralph
  https://theocdstories.com/
- Your Anxiety Toolkit with Kimberley Quinlan, LMFT
  https://kimberleyquinlan-lmft.com/podcast-blog/
- AT Parenting Survival: Raising Kids with OCD & Anxiety with Child Therapist Natasha Daniels
  https://open.spotify.com/show/5TmafYSTYAIFeITSC0ExEi
- Podcast: Welness and Weight Loss Debunked and Decoded
  https://www.maintenancephase.com/
- Food Psych with Christy Harrison MPH, RD, CEDS
  https://christyharrison.com/foodpsych
- Let Us Eat Cake, hosted by registered dietitians Ali Eberhardt and Hannah Robinson
  https://www.letuseatcakepodcast.com/

YouTube

- International OCD Foundation
  https://youtube.com/@iocdf?si=0c0i4Vd10lkG2U3g
- National Alliance for Eating Disorders
  https://youtube.com/@alliancefored?feature=shared
- OCD and Anxiety with Nathan Peterson, therapist and OCD specialist
  https://www.youtube.com/ocdandanxiety
- Dr. Russ Harris—Acceptance Commitment Therapy
  https://www.youtube.com/@dr.russharris-acceptanceco972/featured

- Natasha Daniels—specializing in treatment for children with OCD or anxiety and education for caregivers

  https://www.youtube.com/@childocdtherapist

Books and Workbooks

A list of books for adults, teens, and children with OCD as well as family members

https://iocdf.org/books/

- *Getting Over OCD: A 10-Step Workbook for Taking Back Your Life* by Jonathan S. Abramowitz
- *The ACT Workbook for OCD* by Marisa T. Mazza, PsyD
- *Everyday Mindfulness for OCD* by Jon Hershfield, MFT and Shala Nicely, LPC
- *The Mindfulness Workbook for OCD* by Jon Hershfield, MFT and Tom Corboy, MFT
- *The Self-Compassion Workbook for OCD: Lean Into Your Fear, Manage Difficult Emotions, and Focus on Recovery* by Kimberly Quinlan, LMFT
- *Freedom from Obsessive Compulsive Disorder: A Personalized Recovery Program for Living with Uncertainty* by Jonathan Grayson
- *Stopping the Noise in Your Head* by Reid Wilson, PhD
- *Playing with Anxiety: Casey's Guide for Teens and Kids* by Reid Wilson, PhD, and Lynn Lyons
- *Overcoming Unwanted Intrusive Thoughts* by Sally Winston, PsyD and Martin N. Seif, PhD
- *The Family Guide to Getting Over OCD: Reclaim Your Life and Help Your Loved One* by Jonathan S. Abramowitz
- *Living Well with OCD: Practical Strategies for Improving Your Daily Life* by Jonathan S. Abramowitz
- *Crushing OCD Workbook for Kids: 50 Fun Activities to Overcome OCD with CBT and Exposures* by Natasha Daniels
- *The OCD Workbook for Kids: Skills to Help Children Manage Obsessive Thoughts and Compulsive Behaviors (An Instant Help Book for Parents & Kids)* by Anthony C. Puliafico, PhD, and Joanna A. Robin, PhD
- *Breaking Free of Child Anxiety and OCD: A Scientifically Proven Program for Parents* by Eli R. Lebowitz

- *The Happiness Trap: How to Stop Struggling and Start Living: A Guide to ACT* by Russ Harris
- *Self-Compassion: The Proven Power of Being Kind to Yourself* by Dr. Kristin Neff
- *Life Beyond Your Eating Disorder: Reclaim Yourself, Regain Your Health* by Johanna S. Kandel
- *Make Peace with Food, Banish Body Shame, and Reclaim Joy* by Shana Minei Spence
- *Body Kindness* by Rebecca Scritchfield, RDN
- *Beautiful You: A Daily Guide to Radical Self-Acceptance* by Rosie Molinary
- *How to Nourish Yourself Through an Eating Disorder: Recovery for Adults with the Plate-by-Plate Approach®* by Casey Crosbie, RD, CSSD, and Wendy Sterling, MS, RD, CSSD
- *How to Nourish Your Child Through an Eating Disorder: A Simple, Plate-by-Plate Approach to Rebuilding a Healthy Relationship with Food* by Casey Crosbie, RD, CSSD, and Wendy Sterling, MS, RD, CSSD
- *The Emotional Eating, Chronic Dieting, Binge Eating & Body Image Workbook: A Trauma-Informed, Weight-Inclusive Approach to Make Peace with Food & Reduce Body Shame* by Judith Matz, LCSW, ACSW, Amy Pershing, LMSW, ACSW, CCTP-II, and Christy Harrison, MPH, RD, CEDS

Informational Videos

- Mindset Family Therapy, OCD and the Mind–short explanation on how the OCD mind works
  https://www.youtube.com/watch?v=hIUkN59EtQo
- IOCDF: Jonathan Grayson, Biology of OCD
  https://www.youtube.com/watch?v=b-2fiUXbq_8&list=PLWpyt7M1s8wzE2JuJ7RFtyNqgVZ8O9TGj&index=19
- IOCDF: Jonathan Grayson, OCD in the Brain
  https://www.youtube.com/watch?v=cLg3VIvAnYc&list=PLWpyt7M1s8wzE2JuJ7RFtyNqgVZ8O9TGj&index=22
- IOCDF: Jonathan Grayson, First Step in the Journey of Uncertainty
  https://www.youtube.com/watch?v=UJXH_WWgvv4&list=PLWpyt7M1s8wzE2JuJ7RFtyNqgVZ8O9TGj&index=20

- IOCDF: Jonathan Grayson, Accepting Uncertainty
  https://www.youtube.com/watch?v=Zgy-HSfWigQ

- IOCDF: Ben Eckstein, Parents with a Child with OCD
  https://www.youtube.com/watch?v=BZyEnCp986E&t=11s

- IOCDF: Uncovering OCD: The Truth About Obsessive Compulsive Disorder (IOCDF)
  https://www.youtube.com/watch?v=h1vjxZTALNg

- Cambridge University: Understanding the OCD Brain (video series).
  https://www.youtube.com/c/cambridgeuniversity/search?query=OCD%20brain

References

Academy for Eating Disorders. *Medical Care Standards Committee. Eating Disorders: Critical Points for Early Recognition and Medical Risk Management in the Care of Individuals with Eating Disorders.* Academy for Eating Disorders, 2021. PDF. Accessed April 23, 2024. https://www.aedweb.org/resources/publications/medical-care-standards.

American Psychiatric Association. 2013. *Diagnostic and Statistical Manual of Mental Disorders*. 5th ed. Washington, DC: American Psychiatric Association.

Anxiety and Depression Association of America. Obsessive Compulsive Disorder (OCD). Last modified 2017. https://adaa.org/understanding-anxiety/co-occurring-disorders/obsessive-compulsive-disorder.

Brown, M. L., and C. A. Levinson. 2022. "Core Eating Disorder Fears: Prevalence and Differences in Eating Disorder Fears across Eating Disorder Diagnoses." *International Journal of Eating Disorders* 55, no. 7: 956–965. https://doi.org/10.1002/eat.23728.

Butler, R. M., B. Williams, and C. A. Levinson. 2023. "An Examination of Eating Disorder Fears in Imaginal Exposure Scripts." *Journal of Affective Disorders* 326: 163–167. https://doi.org/10.1016/j.jad.2023.01.121.

Butler, R. M., and R. G. Heimberg. 2020. "Exposure Therapy for Eating Disorders: A Systematic Review." *Clinical Psychology Review* 78: 101851. https://doi.org/10.1016/j.cpr.2020.101851.

Drakes, D. H., E. J. Fawcett, J. P. Rose, J. C. Carter-Major, and J. M. Fawcett. 2021. "Comorbid Obsessive-Compulsive Disorder in Individuals with Eating Disorders: An Epidemiological Meta-Analysis." *Journal of Psychiatric Research* 141: 176–91. https://doi.org/10.1016/j.jpsychires.2021.06.035.

Farrell, N. R., C. Black Becker, and G. Waller. 2019. *Exposure Therapy for Eating Disorders.* New York: Oxford University Press.

Farrell, N. R., C. Black Becker, and G. Waller. 2024. *Eat Without Fear: Harnessing Science to Confront and Overcome Your Eating Disorder.* New York: Oxford University Press.

Glasofer, D. R., A. M. Albano, H. B. Simpson, and J. E. Steinglass. 2016. "Overcoming Fear of Eating: A Case Study of a Novel Use of Exposure and Response Prevention." *Psychotherapy* 53 (2): 223–31. https://doi.org/10.1037/pst0000048.

Grayson, J. *Freedom from Obsessive Compulsive Disorder: A Personalized Recovery Program for Living with Uncertainty*. 2014. Updated edition. New York: Berkley Books.

Harris, R. 2019. *ACT Made Simple: An Easy-to-Read Primer on Acceptance and Commitment Therapy*. 2nd ed. Oakland, CA: New Harbinger.

Harris, R. 2022. *The Happiness Trap: How to Stop Struggling and Start Living.* 2nd ed. Boulder, CO: Shambhala.

Hezel, D. M., S. V. Rose, and H. B. Simpson. 2022. "Delay to Diagnosis in OCD." *Journal of Obsessive-Compulsive and Related Disorders* 32: 100709. https://doi.org/10.1016/j.jocrd.2022.100709.

Kandel, J. 2010. *Life Beyond Your Eating Disorder: Reclaim Yourself, Regain Your Health, and Recover for Good.* New York: Harlequin.

Levin, R. L., J. S. Mills, S. E. McComb, J. S. Rawana. 2023. "Examining Orthorexia Nervosa: Using Latent Profile Analysis to Explore Potential Diagnostic Classification and Subtypes in a Non-Clinical Sample." *Appetite* 181: 106398. https://doi.org/10.1016/j.appet.2022.106398.

Mazza, M. 2020. *The ACT Workbook for OCD: Mindfulness, Acceptance, and Exposure Skills to Live Well with Obsessive-Compulsive Disorder.* Oakland, CA: New Harbinger.

National Institute of Mental Health. 2021. "Obsessive-Compulsive Disorder." Bethesda, MD: National Institutes of Health, https://www.nimh.nih.gov/health/topics/obsessive-compulsive-disorder-ocd.

Neff K. 2011. *Self-Compassion: The Proven Power of Being Kind to Yourself.* 2nd ed. New York: William Morrow Paperbacks.

Storch, E. A., S. A. Rasmussen, L.H. Price, M. J. Larson, T. K. Murphy, and W. K. Goodman. 2010. *The Yale-Brown Obsessive Compulsive Scale–Second Edition (Y-BOCS-II).* San Antonio, TX: Pearson.

Tribole, E., and E. Resch. 2017. *The Intuitive Eating Workbook: Ten Principles for Nourishing a Healthy Relationship with Food.* Oakland, CA: New Harbinger Publications.

Tribole, E., and E. Resch. 2020. *Intuitive Eating: A Revolutionary Anti-Diet Approach.* 4th ed. New York: St. Martin's Press.

Williams, B. M., and C. A. Levinson. 2021. "Intolerance of Uncertainty and Maladaptive Perfectionism as Maintenance Factors for Eating Disorders and Obsessive-Compulsive Disorder Symptoms." *European Eating Disorders Review* 29, no. 1: 101–111. https://doi.org/10.1002/erv.2807.

Zagaria, A., M. Vacca, S. Cerolini, A. Ballesio, C. Lombardo. 2022. "Associations between Orthorexia, Disordered Eating, and Obsessive-Compulsive Symptoms: A Systematic Review and Meta-Analysis." *International Journal of Eating Disorders* 55, no. 3: 295–312. https://doi.org/10.1002/eat.23654.

Lissette Cortes, PsyD, CEDS, is a licensed psychologist in Florida, certified eating disorders specialist, founder of Compassionate Healing Institute, and cofounder of the International OCD Foundation Special Interest Group (IOCDF SIG) for OCD and Eating Disorders. She is a cognitive behavioral psychologist specializing in exposure and response prevention (ERP), and a Health at Every Size (HAES)-aligned clinician practicing from a size-inclusive and diet-rejecting perspective incorporating Intuitive Eating principles. She is on the board of the South Florida iaedp (International Association Of Eating Disorders Professionals Foundation) chapter, and on the board of the CBT Alliance of Florida.

Katie Jeffrey, MS, RDN, CSSD, LDN, is a registered dietitian nutritionist, board-certified specialist in sports nutrition, qualified instructor of mindful eating and living (MB-EAT-QI) through the Mindful Eating Training Institute (METI), and cofounder of the IOCDF SIG for OCD and Eating Disorders. She promotes a weight-neutral, non-diet mindful and intuitive eating and fueling philosophy in her private practice. Katie's mission is to empower individuals to honor their inner wisdom, make peace with food, feel comfortable in their body, cultivate a nourishing self-care practice—and enjoy a lifetime of emotional resiliency by bringing greater awareness, curiosity, and compassion to their behaviors, thoughts, and feelings.

Foreword writer **Nicholas Farrell, PhD**, is a clinical director at NOCD, where he provides leadership and direction for teletherapy services. He is a recognized expert in researching and treating OCD, eating disorders, and other related conditions.

Did you know there are **free tools** you can download for this book?

Free tools are things like **worksheets**, **guided meditation exercises**, and **more** that will help you get the most out of your book.

You can download free tools for this book—whether you bought or borrowed it, in any format, from any source—from the New Harbinger website. All you need is a NewHarbinger.com account. Just use the URL provided in this book to view the free tools that are available for it. Then, click on the "download" button for the free tool you want, and follow the prompts that appear to log in to your NewHarbinger.com account and download the material.

You can also save the free tools for this book to your **Free Tools Library** so you can access them again anytime, just by logging in to your account! Just look for this button on the book's free tools page.

+ Save this to my free tools library

If you need help accessing or downloading free tools, visit **newharbinger.com/faq** or contact us at **customerservice@newharbinger.com.**